# Journeying to
# otherworlds

# Journeying to
# otherworlds

Will Adcock
Rosalind Powell
Anthony Duncan

LORENZ BOOKS

This edition is published by Lorenz Books

Lorenz Books
is an imprint of Anness Publishing Ltd
Hermes House, 88–89 Blackfriars Road
London SE1 8HA
tel. 020 7401 2077; fax 020 7633 9499
www.lorenzbooks.com; info@anness.com

© Anness Publishing Ltd 2004

UK agent: The Manning Partnership Ltd
6 The Old Dairy, Melcombe Road
Bath BA2 3LR
tel. 01225 478444; fax 01225 478440
sales@manning-partnership.co.uk

UK distributor: Grantham Book Services Ltd
Isaac Newton Way, Alma Park Industrial Estate
Grantham, Lincs NG31 9SD
tel. 01476 541080; fax 01476 541061
orders@gbs.tbs-ltd.co.uk

North American agent/distributor: National Book Network
4501 Forbes Boulevard
Suite 200, Lanham, MD 20706
tel. 301 459 3366; fax 301 429 5746
www.nbnbooks.com

Australian agent/distributor: Pan Macmillan Australia
Level 18, St Martins Tower
31 Market St, Sydney, NSW 2000
tel. 1300 135 113; fax 1300 135 103
customer.service@macmillan.com.au

New Zealand agent/distributor: David Bateman Ltd
30 Tarndale Grove, Off Bush Road
Albany, Auckland
tel. (09) 415 7664; fax (09) 415 8892

A CIP catalogue record for this book is available from the
British Library.

Publisher: Joanna Lorenz
Editorial Director: Helen Sudell
Senior Editor: Joanne Rippin
Project Editor: Debra Mayhew
Designers: Ruth Hope, Nigel Partridge
Special Photography: Don Last
Illustrator: Garrry Walton
Production Controller: Darren Price

Previously published in three separate volumes, titles in italics
*Shamanism*, *Dream Therapy*, *Celtic Mysticism*

10 9 8 7 6 5 4 3 2 1

The reader should not regard the recommendations, ideas and
techniques expressed and described in this book as substitutes for
the advice of a qualified medical practitioner or other qualified
professional. Any use to which the recommendations, ideas and
techniques are put is at the reader's sole discretion and risk.

Acknowledgements
The publishers would like to thank the following picture libraries
and photographers for the use of their pictures.
**AKG London**: 18bl and tr; 19, 36br, 37tl, 78bl, 83bl, 84l, 86l, 89tr,
98, 104, 105br, 134br, 146t, 148tl, 149tr, 158, 163tl, 167tl, 174bl,
175bl, 176, 177, 178bl, 180, 182, 183tl, 184t, 188trm 189tl.
**Ancient Art and Architecture**: 36bl, 37br, 38, 40tl, 70, 79, 80tr,
81t and b, 134t, 135tl, 141t, 164. **The Art Archive**: 16tl and br, 17,
52bl, 80l, 83tr, 91, 107r, 140, 146bl. **BBC Natural History Unit**:
60bl, 62bl, 64tl, 65t. **Bridgeman Art Library**: 74tr, 75, 76tr, 85,
96, 109r. **Elizabeth Rees**: 166br. **Fine Art Photographic
Library**: 74br, 90br, 123bl, 147, 154br, 179t, 181br, 186bl, 188bl,
189tr and b. **Images Colour Library**: 27l, 50bl, 56tr and br, 62tr,
65b, 67bl, 89bl, 101tr, 128t, 131tr, 172, 173tl, 175tr, 187br. **Mary
Evans Picture Library**: 138, 139tl and tr, 141br, 142bl and r, 143,
144, 145tl and br, 154tl and tr and bl, 160bl and tr, 161tl and br,
168bl and tr. **Mick Sharp Photography**: 165tl and br, 183br,
185tl, 186tr. **Tony Stone Images**: 22b and tr, 23, 24bl, 27tr, 32b,
56b, 57tl, 58bl and br, 59r, 61tl, and br, 63, 64r, 67t and r, 82t and b,
84r, 88bl, 93tr, 100tr, 107tl, 124tl and tr, 126bl, 129br, 135tr, 148bl
and tr, 151tr and b, 173br, 179bl, 182tr, 187bl. **SuperStock**: 102tr,
123tm, tr and tl, 126bm; 128br. **Werner Forman Archive**: 149br,
162bl, 163tr, 174tr and br. **Wildlife Matters**: 25bl.

# CONTENTS

# INTRODUCTION

*ABOVE: Simple tools help to create the right environment for meditation.*

Physical journeys take us away from home to other places. These may be new and exciting or familiar and comfortable, but along the way we gather new information and experiences that alter our perception of the world around us. A long trip to a far-away country with an entirely different culture to our own can have a profound effect on us, but even a short foray into a new environment nearby can be stimulating.

So it is with journeys of the mind, for we can embark on voyages of self-discovery, exploring aspects of ourselves that were formerly hidden, in search of enlightenment and wisdom. Certainly, as established religion loses its appeal for many modern people, the desire to connect somehow with the natural world is undiminished. Increasing numbers seem to be turning to so-called alternative ways of seeking a truth that provides satisfaction.

## INWARD JOURNEYS

We may follow the shaman's route, travelling first into our personal sacred space and then, as we gain experience, into the realms of the underworld and the upperworld. Shamanism is probably the earliest manifestation of human beings' desire to experience a connection with the universe. We think it was practised by the first hunter-gatherers, perhaps in an effort to influence the world on which they depended, and it is certainly alive today among some societies that live in close harmony with nature. In such groups, the shaman continues to fulfil the traditional role of mediator with the otherworlds, caring for the spiritual wellbeing of the group, accessing useful knowledge and assisting the sick.

Although our urbanized society, in the twenty-first century, is less immediately dependent on the forces of nature or concerned about disgruntled gods, we can still benefit from the personal type of wisdom that can be acquired from shamanistic spiritual travel. With its clear emphasis on personal growth and enlightenment, shamanism has become increasingly attractive to many Western people, and it is practised in a modern way, retaining elements of ritual and using traditional tools, but without some of the extremes of more traditional methods. Anyone with the commitment to succeed will be able to take an inward journey to reach other levels of consciousness. All that is required is a willingness to learn the basic rituals and be guided by spirit animals.

*ABOVE: Being outdoors is a great way to feel connected to the universe.*

## DREAM WORLDS

Throughout history human beings have been intrigued and perturbed by dreams, and the ancients had a number of theories as to their purpose. They were often thought of as attempts by the gods to communicate with mortal beings. Another view was that events in dreams were portents of future events and so needed to be heeded. Aboriginal Australians placed their entire creation story in a dimension referred to as "Dreamtime". With little distinction being made between dreams and waking events, new ceremonies and rituals can be created based on either. Some Buddhists practise lucid dreaming in an effort to define the waking world as well as the dreaming one as illusory and thereby achieve total enlightenment, which will release them from the perpetual cycle of life. To native North Americans dreams are the most important aspect of their lives; they can be good or bad, and rituals may have to be performed as a result of bad ones. In the West, Sigmund Freud and Carl Jung placed great psychological significance on dreams, and as a result, we can now use dream analysis to decipher deep-rooted anxieties or concerns that a dreamer has repressed.

Many people believe that a deeper understanding of our own dreams will help us to know ourselves better. If we can recognize and explain common dream themes (falling, flying, being chased or finding oneself in an embarrassing

*ABOVE: The shaman's tools are few and simple.*

situation) and if we know the underlying meaning of universal dream symbols, we will be better equipped to interpret our own dreams, thus gaining deeper insight into our own minds. By keeping an open mind about interpreting our dreams, we will probably have greater success in learning something useful from them. Alternatively, we can learn to simply appreciate our dreams as something enjoyable, although we are likely to want to know the causes of our troubling nightmares so that we can eliminate them and enjoy more restful sleep.

## CELTIC MYSTICISM

With a holistic worldview that acknowledges the cyclic nature of existence and sees the sacred and the secular as one, it is hardly surprising that the Celtic approach to life continues to appeal. Dating back to pre-Roman times, its rich myths and legends celebrate the interconnectedness of life and the natural world. Tapping into this rich energy gives the spiritual traveller a sense of being part of something wonderful and opens their eyes to a new way of seeing.

Traditionally, Druids, or seers, had intimate knowledge of the natural world and were the keepers of wisdom. Today it is still possible for such practitioners to travel to Annwn, the Otherworld, in search of knowledge. Access to Annwn is gained through gateways that will be revealed once a journey has begun.

On such a shamanic voyage, the traveller may come across obstacles that must be overcome, but helpers in the form of spirits or gods will be there to assist. Archetypical figures from the myths, which are, in reality, aspects of ourselves, are often encountered and may teach us rather more than we expected to learn. An experienced traveller will also be able to shift-shape along the way if necessary.

## ABOUT THIS BOOK

Gathered together in this book is a wealth of information about three effective routes for spiritual travel. Divided into eight chapters, they contain all you need to know about

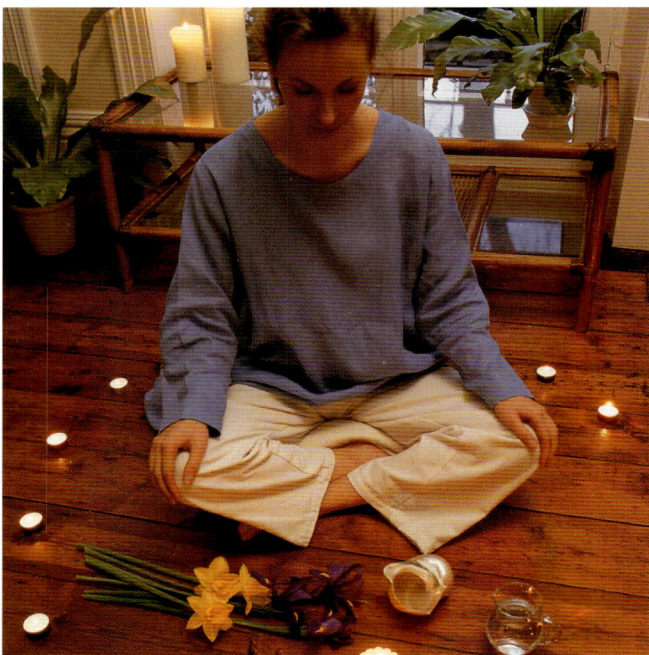

shamanism, the world of dreams and the Celtic worldview to enable you to start on your own journey towards self-awareness, personal growth and enlightenment.

## THE WORLD OF THE SHAMAN

The first three chapters provide practical insight into the fascinating world of the shaman and show how to work with nature to achieve your goals. All the essential techniques are covered, including visualization, using symbols, herbs and incense, altering the atmosphere, making altars and stone circles, and smudging (cleansing an aura). So too is an explanation of the tools – physical and mental – that you will need for your travels.

Sacred space – mental or physical – is the crucial starting point for your spiritual journeys, so your first task will be to learn how to make such a space. Ritual helps to focus on a particular act, thereby increasing its efficacy as well as strengthening our connection with the universe. It can have far-reaching effects, and everyday activities such as greeting the morning, eating, breathing or making an offering in thanks can all be enhanced when performed in a certain way.

Several tools, especially the drum with its primal undertones, are of great importance. Once these have been acquired or made, and you understand their use, you will be ready to start journeying. On your first journey you are likely to meet your personal spirit or power animal. Learn how to recognize it, and it will be there to accompany you on further journeys of self-discovery. You will also learn how to travel beyond a sacred space into the realms of the underworld and the upperworld. The first equates with

*LEFT: Choose a quiet time of day to meditate.*

8

the inner recesses of the mind; it is a place of challenges and adventure, where you can confront you own fears. The second is the upperworld, which is associated with the higher self or soul; light and tranquil, it is where you go to seek inspiration and information and to commune and share knowledge with other spirits.

## LEARNING ABOUT DREAMS

The next two chapters of the book show how you can to explore dreams in a meaningful way in order to gain personal insight and so help cope better with life. It examines the purpose of sleep and dreams, as well as any associated deep-rooted psychology. It gives practical suggestions for ensuring a good night's sleep in order to help dreams flourish, and suggests ways to record dreams before they melt away from memory.

Once you have recorded your dreams, you will be able to analyse them and start to make some sense out of them. Common themes have meanings that may not be obvious at first sight, and learning how to read universal dream symbols in the light of your own personal situation will also make your interpretations more pertinent to you. It is possible to influence your dreams in an attempt to solve a particular problem, come up with new ideas, make decisions, or simply to have some fun. While the ancients practised this skill in a number of ways that would not be practical today, here you will find more useful suggestions to try.

*ABOVE: The tools to cleanse a room.*

*ABOVE: Herbs and spices are used by the shaman.*

## ENGAGING WITH NATURE

The Celtic world is rich in complex myths that show how human beings are inseparable from the natural and spiritual world around them. Anyone who feels drawn to this holistic worldview needs to learn something of the Celtic mind. The closing three chapters of this book comprise a comprehensive introduction to the subject: explanations about the Great, or Earth, Mother and the male god Dagda, stories of Morrighan and Brigit, and tales of Arthur illustrate the mysterious, mystical world of the Celts. With these in mind, the spiritual traveller will be better equipped to commune with nature and embark on journeys. This practical information will set you on your way to seeking inner silence, communing with nature, travelling to the Otherworld and meeting up with archetypes through meditation.

# SHAMANISM

# SHAMANISM

The old man's breath came in white puffs as he chanted softly, almost inaudibly, in his slowly spinning progression around the wheel, circles within a circle. He had been dancing and chanting for hours and now, as he sensed the climax of the ritual, his spinning became more animated, whirling him around the circle he had created with his stamping feet. In a triumphant finale he scooped a double armful of snow from the eastern gateway and hurled it skywards, watching the uppermost ice crystals catch the light of the returning sun. Arms raised aloft, the shaman greeted the beginning of the sunrise that heralded the end of the long winter night.

Shamanism is essentially a state of mind a way of viewing life as a whole. The shaman gains insights and wisdom by connecting with other parts of creation and healing the divisions that exist between the separate pieces. Such divisions can occur anywhere: within the self, within groups, between people and the environment, and so on.

The word shaman comes from the Tungusic dialect of the Ural-Altaic tribes of Siberia. Shamans were the priest-doctors of the tribes, responsible for officiating at ceremonies and rituals, tending the sick and caring for all aspects of the spiritual wellbeing of the people.

Shamanism does not recognize age, gender, race or religious doctrines and so is available to all. Indeed, many people have shamanic experiences without labelling them as such. It could even be said that some important scientific discoveries have been instigated by shamanic experiences. Humans are a part of creation and shamanism is our way of connecting with the whole. It is a fundamental part of our heritage and, although the connection may be weakened by modern life, the ability to connect, and the inclination to do so, is still present. This chapter is an introduction to shamanic practices, it will guide you towards wisdom through rituals, journeying, and working with dreams.

RIGHT: A Shaman's journey begins with the beat of the drum.

# THE SHAMAN'S ROUTE

Rooted in the primeval beliefs of early humans and still practised by societies living in close harmony with nature, shamanism has increasing resonance for many Westerners seeking spiritual growth and enlightenment. Traditional shamans were, and still are, essential intermediaries with the spirits that govern every aspect of the natural world and therefore the lot of humankind. Their ability to connect with the universe imbues them with powerful knowledge that equips them to interpret events, influence the outcome of strategies for survival, give guidance and heal the sick and wounded. Modern practitioners of shamanism use insights gained during their travels to help them grow spiritually.

# THE TRADITION OF THE SHAMAN

*ABOVE: A Kamchatka shaman dancing with a drum.*

When communities were much more isolated and self-reliant than modern society is, shamans played an integral part in their cultures, performing numerous and specific duties. They practised healing in cases of sickness and injury, but they were not specifically healers. Although they communed with ancestors, spirits and gods, they were not exclusively priests, and while they offered wise counsel to their communities, they were not solely sages. Rather, they fulfilled a combination of these roles and several others besides.

## THE SHAMAN'S ROLE

To understand the function of a shaman, it is necessary to adopt a world view relative to traditional peoples. Typically, older cultures more in touch with the natural world have been animistic societies. Animism is a term derived from the Latin anima, which means soul, and these older cultures held the belief that all things possessed a soul or spirit. The fundamental role of the shaman was to act as an intermediary in relating to the other spirits of the earth: the animals, the land, the rain, the crops and so on. Because humans were so dependent on the forces of nature and the other beings of the planet, communicating with them was seen as a way of predicting problems or finding a way out of them. The shaman could send his or her soul out on a journey to meet with these other spirits and ensure a successful hunt or determine why a crop was failing, or if there would be a drought. These journeys of the soul could also lead shamans to other dimensions where they would commune with gods, find special

*ABOVE: A North American blackfoot shaman in ceremonial robes.*

knowledge or acquire powers that gave them an advantage when living in difficult times or healing the sick and injured.

It was this ability to travel at will to other realms that marked out the shaman. Very often it was unlooked for, with visions occurring spontaneously, or caused by traumatic experiences such as severe illness or injury. What is often termed "madness" in modern western society was seen as being "touched by the gods" by traditional people. Shamans usually lived somewhat apart from the rest of the community, because their powers made them different from other people. However, individuals who were able to hear voices and experience realities beyond the normal scope of perception were naturally regarded with respect and awe.

## SHAMANIC JOURNEYING

These altered states of consciousness could also be induced by a shaman seeking to go on a journey. The drum was a very powerful shamanic tool, seen as a mode of transporting the soul on its regular beat as it opened gateways for the shaman. Dancing was another method employed to achieve a trance state, usually to contact a specific animal spirit. By moving the body in a way that mimicked the animal in question, the shaman became that animal and was able to relate directly to it. Costume was also important in this respect and the use of feathers, skins, bones and significant designs was seen as a way of linking with spirits and journeying to other dimensions.

Sacred plants have a long history of being used as a means of accessing the spirit worlds. In Europe, fly agaric, psilocybe mushrooms and doses of hemlock were all used as vehicles by which a shaman could enter an altered state of consciousness. In Mexico, the peyote cactus was, and still is, eaten in a ritual that takes many hours to unfold. The trance state it induces brings the shaman into contact with the spirit of the universe, who grants visions and bestows knowledge.

In South America the principal sacred plant is the banisteriopsis vine, which has also been used for a long time. The plant is brewed into a drink known as ayahuasca or

ABOVE: *Animal skins helped a shaman commune with the spirits.*

yagé, which is drunk during a ceremony. It produces similar effects to those of peyote, inducing visionary trances and heightened telepathic abilities which allow the shaman to "tune in" to the different levels of creation or travel to otherworlds.

Because of the powers of these sacred plants, they need to be approached with respect. Their gathering and preparation involves a lengthy ritual incorporating prayers and offerings to the spirits of the plants that can take many hours or even last for days.

Shamans, then, held a position of influence but also one of great responsibility. The people would turn to them first in matters of importance, and the shamans would use their abilities and powers to find a satisfactory outcome to the problems of the day.

## LEGENDARY SHAMANS

In the European cultures there are many myths of shamans and shamanic adventures. Ceridwen was a great Celtic shaman who brewed a magic potion to confer infinite knowledge on her son. However, it was inadvertently tasted by her kitchen boy, who thus acquired all her wisdom. During a shapeshifting chase to catch him, she became a hen and he a grain of corn. Ceridwen ate the corn and

*ABOVE: Merlin dictates his history.*

became pregnant with the Celtic bard, Taliesin.

In the Arthurian legends, Merlin possessed divinatory powers and could shapeshift, commune with animals and spirits and travel to the otherworlds.

Odin, the chief god of the Aesir in the Scandinavian Pantheon, was another famous shaman. He gave up one of his eyes in return for a drink from the well of Mimir, the water of which was the source of all wisdom. He also sacrificed himself on the World Tree to learn the wisdom of the dead, bringing back runes from the underworld.

## MODERN SHAMANISM

Traditional shamanism still exists in many places in the world, especially where the old cultures remain strong. It is not uncommon for people to seek the assistance of a shaman in the lands of the Arctic, Africa, Australasia, Indonesia, North and South America, Mongolia, China and Tibet.

Although in modern western societies there seems to be little need for a shaman to help with problems about food shortages, destructive weather or disgruntled gods, there is nonetheless a place for shamanism on a more personal level. Shamanism is a way to find our place in the vast universe. By embarking upon a shamanic journey to other levels of consciousness, the modern shaman can reach depths, or heights, of insight that can eventually lead to personal growth and enlightenment.

*ABOVE: The young Arthur receives teaching from Merlin.*

*RIGHT: One-eyed Odin on his magical steed, Sleipnir.*

# Tapping into Spirit

The spirit of creation is present in all life and matter, connected by a web of energy. Each part of this universal web vibrates at its own frequency, and over the millennia human beings have discovered many ways to tap into the web in search of enlightenment and fulfilment. Among these routes are creating sacred space, communing and working with nature, visualization techniques, and the use of altars, stone circles and symbols. Further aids for rewarding inward travel include acts of physical and spiritual purification using certain herbs and incense, simple daily rituals that increase the efficacy of our acts, and making offerings of gratitude.

# CONNECTING WITH SPIRIT

What is spirit? How can it be defined? Spirit is the omnipresent energy possessed by all things. It is the essence of creation, the unifying force that is present throughout the universe. Spirit connects us one with another, but also with animals, plants, rocks, water, air, the stars and the space between the stars. It is the skein of being beyond the physical that can be accessed for communication, for healing and for understanding.

Imagine a spider's web, a beautifully delicate construction designed to catch flies and transmit vibrations. The structure is continuous, so that the whole is affected to some degree wherever an insect is trapped in it. Moreover, the spider can differentiate between the struggling of a trapped fly and the vibration set up by, say, the wind or an airborne seed. The simile of a web is used in many traditional societies to illustrate the principle of connectedness, and the same analogy is used in the modern world – in the World Wide Web, the information super-highway, which permits worldwide communication in virtually no time at all. Just think of the energy incorporated here – energy that is an extension of the universal energy, the spirit of creation.

Of course, the universal connection is far more complex than the tracery created by a single spider, intricate as this is, or even the myriad connections of the internet, because there are webs within webs. The spirit web of the human race is made up of smaller webs of friends and family; the

*ABOVE: A spider's web illustrates connectedness.*

spiritual web of life on Earth is an amalgamation of humans, animals, plants, rocks and water.

The fundamental link in the web is energy. Energy suffuses all things, but the energy of each part of creation vibrates at its own particular frequency. The energy encompassed by any entity, be it a rock, a blade of grass, an animal or a human being, is simply an extension of the web of spirit, and the extent to which you as an individual can affect and be affected by communication on the universal network depends upon how receptive you are.

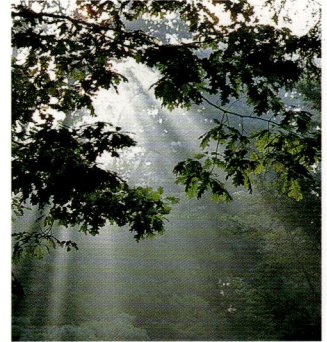

*ABOVE: Energy is apparent all around us.*

All of us are aware of energy on an instinctive level. We have all experienced atmospheres; in a room after an argument has occurred, for instance, so much energy has been emitted that the air is thick with it. On a more subtle level, there is the instinctive feeling that you are liked or disliked by someone. Because humans have closely linked vibrations, the energy is usually readily sensed by other humans when you meet. Similarly, a shaman can extend this sensitivity to feel the vibrations of other parts of creation.

*ABOVE: The night sky is a potent reminder of the universality of creation.*

# SACRED SPACE

There are many examples of sacred sites around the world that have special significance to particular societies: Stonehenge for the Druids; Mount Olympus for the Greeks; the San Francisco Mountains for the native American Zuni tribe; the Black Hills of South Dakota for the plains tribes; and Uluru (formerly known as Ayers Rock) for the Australian tribes. These sites are usually ancient and powerful places associated with the ancestors, gods or spirits of a given culture. They are important to the collective psyche of the society. Sacred space approaches the concept on a more personal level.

Is there a place that you find especially conducive to meditation or relaxation? Perhaps a beneath a tree in a park or your garden, a certain rock outcrop in the vicinity, or a wood where you often walk. Anywhere that you feel comfortable sitting alone can be a sacred space, and that includes a place within yourself; sometimes it's not possible to travel physically to a special place to unwind just when you need to, so why not carry it with you?

The inner sacred space is a place that you create as a sanctuary, a retreat from the physical world, where you can relax and recoup your energy, so it can resemble anything that makes you feel comfortable: a desert island, a hut on a mountain, a cave, anything. Maybe it's a place that you already know; somewhere you have visited in a dream or in this world. The more you visualize, the more real it will seem, so try to feel textures, see details, hear sounds and smell scents.

*ABOVE: Your sacred space is a safe, secure place.*

Your sacred space is a safe place and, because it is always there, you can visit it at any time you choose. It can evolve in detail as much as you want it to, because you created it and the control over it lies only with you. The only limitations are ones that you, as the maker, impose. So, be aware of what comes into being, for that can offer important insights into your subconscious. This private place is a good jumping-off point for beginning journeys.

*LEFT: Stonehenge in Wiltshire, England, is an ancient sacred site for the Druids.*

## EXPERIENCING NATURE

The natural world is a great place to find peace, tranquillity and inspiration, and to practise visualizing details to put into your own sacred space. Get out as much as possible to experience the benefits that a natural environment can bring. When out walking, be aware of your surroundings, admire the beauty of a tree or a bird in flight and always be grateful. Life is a precious gift to be appreciated now.

Nature can give us many things to help remind us of our connection – stones, feathers, sticks, intricate patterns and images – but if anything is taken, remember to leave something in return as an offering, an exchange of energy to signify your appreciation of the gift that has been given to you. Shamanism is about relating to the natural world and our place in it. Take time to stop, relax and meditate on the incredible complexity of the creation around you. Close your eyes and see how much sharper your other senses become. Extend that receptivity to feel the land, and blend with it. Feel what is around you: the vitality of the earth, the immensity of the world and the universe beyond. You are a part of it, be aware and accept the experience for what it is: humbling and precious.

*ABOVE: Practising shamanism in a natural setting enhances the bond between you and the world around you.*

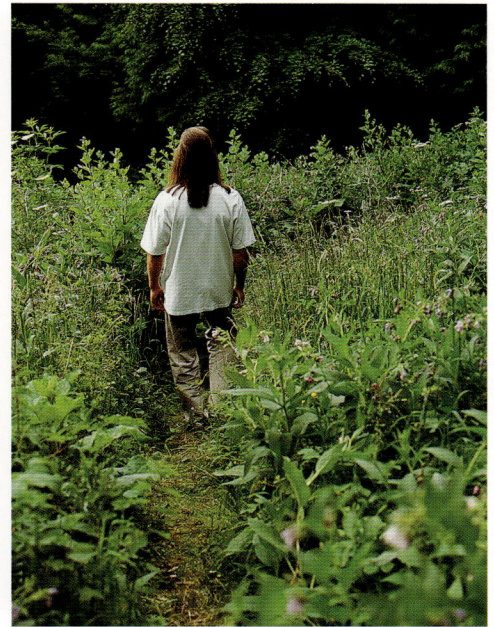

*ABOVE: Regular visits to the countryside help to connect you with other parts of creation.*

# VISUALIZING SACRED SPACE

Before you begin journeying or dreamwork you need to work on visualizing a place in your mind that becomes your own personal sacred space. The sacred space you create will be your place and only people you invite may enter. It can be any kind of place in which your spirit feels happy and at home: a woodland clearing, a cave, a deserted beach, even a corner of your own garden. The more times you visit your sacred space the more real it will seem and the easier it will be to get there. Concentrate on creating and remembering detail; love the place, care for it, plant flowers and trees and tend them as they grow, decorate it as you would your home. Work out rituals for arriving and leaving and, from time to time, imagine making an offering there to help express your gratitude.

## ENTERING YOUR SACRED SPACE

Use these steps to build and enter your sacred space. As with all shamanic practices it is good to begin with a calm state of mind. Breathe from your diaphragm and release any worries. When you feel relaxed, picture your spirit body stepping out of your physical body. Your spirit body is beautiful, glowing, solid and real, connected to your earthly body by a thin filament. Look down at yourself, sitting or lying peacefully, before you start the journey.

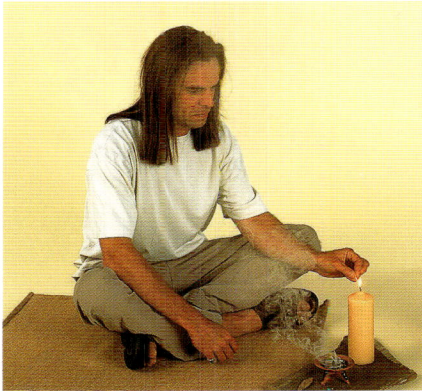

**1** Take five deep breaths to centre yourself and focus your mind on what you are about to do. Voice your intent out loud. Light a candle and burn some incense, holding your intention in your mind.

**2** Contemplate the candle flame for a while, imagining it lighting up the recesses inside you so that you may find a way to the place you seek more easily.

**3** When you feel ready to start, sit or lie down comfortably, somewhere you won't be disturbed, and focus on your breathing. With closed eyes, take deep, slow breaths from your diaphragm to keep relaxed.

## EXPANDING THE VISUALIZATION

Now picture an opening: a natural doorway such as a hole in the ground or the mouth of a cave. This will lead you to the sacred space you seek. When you pass through, pay attention to details that will make the place seem more real.

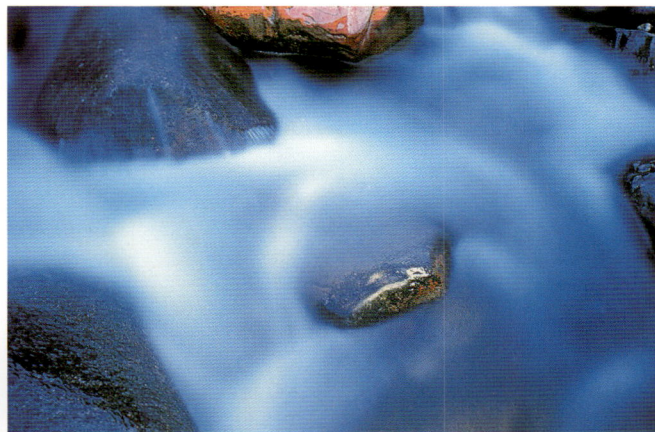

ABOVE: *Use all your senses to make the place as real as possible.*

ABOVE: *The entrance to your personal space could be a cave.*

Utilize all your senses to give the place solidity. This is tricky, but with a bit of practice it will get easier.

Expand your senses. Touch trees and feel the texture of the bark; sit on a rock and feel its surface – is it smooth or rough? Feel the warmth of the sun as you walk through the place. What is beneath your feet? Grass, sand, a path? Pause to smell the delicate fragrance of a flower, the bloom redolent with

its essence of attraction. Look into it and notice how bright the colours are and how the petals and stamens are arranged. Hear the birdsong and the sighing of the wind. Sit by a stream, taste the refreshing coolness of the water and absorb the beauty and peace.

When you feel it is time to leave, give thanks and promise to return. Retrace your steps through the entrance, back your physical body. Come slowly back to this world.

ABOVE: *Picture the smallest and most intricate detail.*

27

# CREATING SACRED SPACE

When dedicating an area or room to a sacred space, it is important to ensure that the atmosphere feels right. A room that formerly had a more functional purpose, like an office or a play area, may have acquired a busy atmosphere over the years, which can affect physically sensitive people who are trying to relax or meditate. The atmosphere will not necessarily be negative, but rather full of misplaced echoes of former thought-forms, each with a residual power of subliminal persuasion.

Transmuting one positive atmosphere into another can be done with a ritual in which you begin by focusing on the old atmosphere, and then swing your focus to the new atmosphere you wish to create. This effectively stamps a new psychic impression upon a place.

### YOU WILL NEED

altar

white candle

3 appropriately coloured candles (different colours emit different resonances)

rose geranium essential oil and burner

4 small tumbled rose quartz crystals

small token of the original use of the space

small token of the new atmosphere

black cloth large enough to cover or contain the first token

*ABOVE: Focus your attention on the task in hand. Do not allow other thoughts to interrupt your concentration.*

*ABOVE: Candles are an important tool in helping to change the atmosphere of a room.*

### THE RITUAL

Set up an altar in the middle of the room. Put the white candle in the centre of the altar with the three coloured candles arranged in a triangle around it. Put a few drops of essential oil in the saucer of the burner and light the burner. Put everything you are going to use in the ritual on the altar for a few moments, then take the rose quartz crystals and put one in each corner of the room.

Take the object you have chosen to represent the old atmosphere, and place it in the western quarter of the room. Take the object that represents the new atmosphere of the room and place it in the eastern quarter. Light all the candles. Start the ritual at the east side of the altar, facing the west. Take a few deep, calming breaths and say the following words.

*Go! Depart! Begone ye hence!*
*Avaunt I say, this is my will!*

*Be ended, finished, changed, transposed,*
*Leave no disturbing echoes still!*

ABOVE: *Clapping hands helps to disperse stagnant energy in a room.*

Clap your hands loudly, then take the black cloth over to the object in the west and cover it. Return to the altar, but this time stand at the west side facing east, in the opposite direction to the earlier part of the ritual. Say these words.

*Now welcome be, now welcome stay, now welcome is for evermore!*
*Be started, newborn, fresh, unfurled,*
*And bring thy presence to the fore!*

Go to the object in the east that represents the new atmosphere and bring it reverentially to the altar to place it there. Sit beside the altar and leave the item there for several minutes while you meditate on it. As you do so, absorb the new atmosphere that is emerging in the room and reflect it back at the object.

When you feel this is complete and the atmosphere has been altered, close the ritual by extinguishing the candles. Dismantle the altar and remove the object that represented the old atmosphere from the room. Leave the object that represents the new atmosphere in a prominent position on a window sill or shelf.

ABOVE: *The tools of space clearing.*

## CLAPPING HANDS

Like any loud and sudden noise, clapping the hands serves to alert and charge the atmosphere. It has the effect of startling a room's energies into an awakened and expectant state.

## CANDLE COLOURS

Choose from the following colours to enhance the atmosphere in your sacred place.

Green: relaxation, harmony, balance, calm.

Blue: peace, calm, relaxation.

Purple: depth, reflection, authority, contemplation.

# ALTARS

We're all familiar with altars, and the term probably conjures up some richly decorated object that may be seen in a temple or a church, but of course they don't have to be like that. Altars serve primarily to focus the attention, so big, brightly coloured ones are good for large places. A small personal altar, using something like a stone or a log, can be placed in your home or garden and will serve the same purpose for you. It needn't be showy, although bright colours have a greater impact on the subconscious, and therefore a greater power.

Altars can be adorned with anything that has a special significance to the user, such as crystals, feathers, flowers or sticks. An altar is also a place to leave offerings. The rituals of decorating and making offerings help to reinforce your connection with the universe; the intent is paramount and the conscious reiteration reminds the physical self of the bond.

*ABOVE: A simple indoor altar.*

## INDOOR ALTARS

An altar can be made using a flat rock or a piece of wood or a small table. Whatever you use, look after it, keep it clean and give it your attention for a few minutes each day. This will help you focus your awareness and strengthen your own spiritual connections.

## NATURAL ALTARS

You may come across a special place when out walking, such as a tree or a rock, which you can use as a temporary altar on which to celebrate that particular moment in time. Being in a more public place, it also has the advantage that others might see it and add their energy to the place.

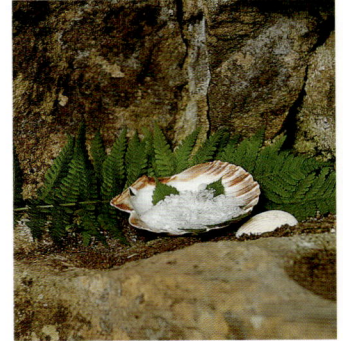

*ABOVE: Altars outside can also be seen by others.*

*ABOVE: Natural altars can show appreciation for the moment.*

Trees make very beautiful natural altars, pleasing to the eye and very calming when attention is focused upon them. Being firmly rooted, a tree has a deep connection with Mother Earth and that energy can be tapped into when you talk to it, leave offerings and pray or meditate there. You can tie things in the branches for decoration, or place tiny items in the trunk. A flat rock placed at the base of the trunk can serve as an altarstone. Be aware of which trees attract you, because they all have their own attributes and symbolism. For example, oak is the keeper of wisdom and possesses great strength; willow represents love and regeneration: being able to grow a new tree from a cut branch; the very tall and graceful beech symbolizes aspirations to higher ideals; yew, associated with ancient burial sites, represents transformation and inner wisdom.

Rocks are the bones of the Mother, supporting her and therefore us. Because they take millions of years to form, they hold ancient Earth wisdom and knowledge, power and strength. They aid in connecting with the Earth because they are so much a part of it, being formed deep within. Call upon this strength when you pray at a rock altar and feel it helping you, supporting you and connecting you.

## MAKING A CAIRN

The beauty of making something to use as an altar is that the maker's energy is blended with the materials in a focused way. A cairn looks like a haphazard pile of stones but, to make it stable, care must be taken in selecting stones that fit together well. Take your time as you gather the stones and lay them.

**1** Begin by selecting a few large, flat, roughly circular rocks that will stack easily, to act as the base of the cairn.

**2** Start to build up a tapering dome by placing smaller flat rocks in an overlapping pattern on top of the base.

**3** As you work, keep the intent of honouring creation in your thoughts, and that will help focus your energy.

**4** When the cairn is complete, decorate it with objects found close by.

## STONE CIRCLES

There are many examples of these ancient structures, especially in the British Isles and other parts of Northern Europe. The full purposes for their construction are unclear, although they are accurate astronomical calendars in which certain stones align with celestial bodies at significant times of the year, such as the summer and winter solstices. In North America there are large circles outlined in stone, at a number of sites. These wheels are orientated to the compass and constructed on sacred sites where people still come to pray and leave offerings.

*ABOVE: The intent behind ancient stone circles is obscure, but they have a simple, awe-inspiring majesty such as this one at Castlerigg, Cumbria, England.*

## MAKING A STONE CIRCLE

Create a sacred space to honour the circle of life and your place in it with your own stone circle. Select seven stones, one each for the four directions, one for Mother Earth, one for the spirit and one for the self.

**1** Bless and place the direction stones first, beginning with the east. Each of the directions has its own symbolism and energy.

**2** Bless each stone before you lay it in place. Put the three remaining stones inside the circle formed by the four direction stones.

**3** The completed stone circle can be used as an altar: as a place to pray, and to give thanks and gain insights into the progression of your life-path.

### BLESSING THE STONES

The **east** is the place of illumination, the place of conception. It is the direction represented by spring with all its vigorous new growth. Call on this energy as you bless the stone and place it in the east position.

The **south** is the place of consolidation, the place of the child. It is the direction represented by summer when the burgeoning life progresses into fullness. Call on this energy as you bless the stone and place it in the south position.

The **west** is the place of fruition, the place of the adult. It is associated with autumn when the growth reaches its ripeness. Call on this energy as you bless the stone and place it in the west position.

The **north** is the place of calm reflection, the place of the elder. It is represented by winter, the season when the strength is drawn in. When the growth cycle is past, the elder has the wisdom of experience to reflect upon. Call upon this energy as you bless the stone and place it in the north position.

The stone for **Mother Earth** is to honour her and thank her for the gifts she gives, the food and shelter she provides, the air she breathes into us and the water that supports us. Recognize her and give thanks as you bless the stone and place it in the circle at the 11 o'clock position, near the centre.

The stone for the **spirit** is to honour and give thanks for all of creation of which we humans are a part. Recognize the bond as you bless the stone and place it in the circle at the one o'clock position, near the centre.

The stone for the **self** is to acknowledge the individual's part in the whole and to give thanks for all the things that come to you. Honour the connection as you bless the stone and place it in the circle at the six o'clock position, near the centre.

# USING AN ALTAR

Although your spiritual journey is an inward one, a sacred place serves as a reminder of the way, and each time you use it you strengthen the positive energy it holds for you.

You may think of your altar as a private place, where you can go to be quiet and restore your calm and inner strength. Use it to nourish your soul and help you unwind. At difficult times of transition use it as a support, and at times of peace, use it to give thanks. If you share the altar with someone else, the times when you are together will reinforce your bond.

*ABOVE: A simple arrangement of meaningful objects keeps the intent of your altar clear.*

## PREPARATION AND CLOSING

Before ceremonies, purify your sacred space by cleaning the room and clearing away clutter, and cleanse yourself so that you feel refreshed and energized. Make sure that the altar is clean and free of dust, that the flowers are fresh and candles new. Burn some incense or white sage to clear away any negative energy from the area.

It is a good idea to devise a formal beginning for your time before the altar: light a candle or some incense to quiet your thoughts and prepare yourself to concentrate all your energy on the subject of your meditation or prayer. Focusing on deep, relaxed breathing helps to still your mind.

Adopt a way of closing your ceremony that you can repeat each time. Playing a piece of music, saying a farewell prayer, "thank you", or simply "amen", will give you a feeling of completion.

## DAILY RITUAL

A small morning ritual is a positive way to start a new day, and doing it before an altar sanctifies the act. If you practise yoga, for instance, performing your salutation to the sun in your sacred space will strengthen your spiritual bond with creation. You can change the format of your worship freely, as your needs and ideas change: you might wish to read a text that inspires you, or recite a poem that helps you express your emotions. Singing, striking a singing bowl, playing a musical instrument or listening to music could form part of your ritual.

*ABOVE: Using flowers as offerings is a simple way to introduce nature.*

If you say daily prayers, or spend a particular period of time in meditation, your altar can become the focus of these regular practices. Prayer and meditation are complementary routes to spiritual development. As a request for help or guidance, or as thanksgiving, prayer is active, while meditation is a passive exercise in contemplation, quieting the mind to increase its receptivity, and allow the subconscious to surface.

Using an affirmation can help to focus your meditation. Create a thought that feels right to you; it needn't describe your present reality, but the reality you dream of. The affirmation is a way to make your dream real. Repeat the positive thought again and again, silently or aloud, to allow it to sink into your unconscious mind.

Place an offering on your altar as an expression of gratitude for the blessings of your life. Leaving a gift for another person on the altar for a while before you give it will endow it with positive energy and reinforce its value.

*ABOVE: Keep crystals clean for positive energy.*

35

# SYMBOLS

*Firelight flickered across the walls of the cave as the shaman sought for a place where the symbol belonged. The dancing shadows played over the frieze of figures already depicted; simple delineations that nevertheless showed the beasts in awesome depth. Aurochs stood four-square with the majestic sweep of their horns held high, horses galloped in a swirl of graceful lines, eagles swooped on widespread wings. And somewhere amongst all these forms was a site for the symbol from last night's dream. Somewhere …There! Taking brush in hand, the shaman approached and began to paint.*

Rock art – paintings in caves and under overhangs, etchings on cliffs and boulders – can be found all over the world, from Europe to Africa, America to China. The pictures span a great length of time, the oldest so far discovered being dated at more than 35,000 years old. They are all symbols that inspired the cultures that they relate to.

Before writing was developed, important information was passed on orally, but our ancestors also used symbolic representations to reinforce aspects of their lives. In this way, pictures of hunting scenes acted as positive visualizations for the successful outcome of a hunt, or as a record of an event, as well as honouring the animals and their importance. Pictures of crops were positive visualizations of good harvests as well as a recognition of the gifts of the Earth. Certain symbols, such as masks or totems, were boundary markers for a particular

*RIGHT: Cave painting of an aurochs, Spain.*

*LEFT: Human figures.*

*ABOVE: Galloping horse, Lascaux cave painting.*

that conveys a wealth of meaning simply and succinctly.

People have used symbols for millennia, as charms for luck, protection, health and inspiration. A symbol has its own energetic vibration and this is what influences the spirit. In the rock art of the ancestors, there are certain symbols that appear in many ancient places around the world, and from many different periods, indicating their fundamental universal importance for the human spirit. Among these powerful signs, or sigils, are the spiral and the circle in their various forms.

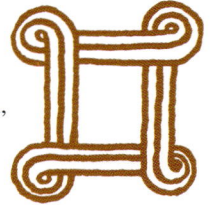

group of people. Other rock art scenes show human figures with animal characteristics such as antlers and wings: these are representative of shapeshifting in shamanic journeys, where a shaman will adopt another form for learning, healing or communication. Some cave art shows the ritual acting out of day-to-day activities such as hunting, with human figures that could be shamanic taking part. Such paintings indicate the antiquity of shamanism.

Even today, a modern version of rock art can be seen in urban settings. The graffiti seen on so many concrete cliffs are symbols that have significance, to their makers at least. Modern symbolism doesn't stop there, though. Think of all the various symbols that surround us: from national flags to advertising logos, religious icons to currency signs, and club insignia, each one a symbol

*ABOVE: A Lascaux cave painting of a human figure, possibly a shaman, taking part in a hunting ritual.*

## SPIRALS AND CIRCLES

The spiral is an evocative image, symbolic of a life path, the lessons and learning that come to an individual through their life. A spiral is formed by tracing a point that is moving simultaneously out and around. The circular motion relates to the cyclic nature of existence, and the outward motion to the spiritual and emotional growth of a person as they progress through life, apparently repeating experiences, but each time moving to a new level.

Sometimes, spirals are combined to make double or even triple forms. Double spirals symbolize the duality of life and the natural world, seen in abundant pairs of complementary opposites, such as light and dark, young and old, mind and body – the spiritual and physical.

In Celtic lore, the triple spiral relates to the three stages of life: maiden, mother and crone. This symbol displays the cycles that are present within cycles, showing that the whole is made up of different periods of growth and development but that each stage is directly linked to the others. The spiral is also representative of a pathway, usually downwards and inwards, that a shaman may take to reach another realm.

Another spiral form, especially prevalent in the Celtic tradition and still seen even today, is the spiral maze, which has the same symbolism as the more ordinary design, that of learning wisdom through initiation and experience.

*RIGHT: The Celtic triple spiral related to the three stages of life: maiden, mother and crone.*

The circle is the line without end. It represents birth, death and rebirth, all intimately linked. For one cycle to begin another must end, but they are not really beginning and ending, merely transmuting.

The circle symbolizes the cycles which are present in all of creation, the relentless progress of life in all its forms. Many traditional dwellings reflected this and were of circular construction, symbolizing living within the whole. Circles that incorporate another solid circle inside, speak of the totality of creation, showing that all things are connected and that creation encompasses the individual.

*ABOVE: Sunburst design showing an arrow-headed spirit line.*

*ABOVE: A medicine wheel simply marked out in stones.*

The sunburst with a spirit line inside it is another circular symbol, evoking the image of the creative essence of the universe breathing life into all things.

## MEDICINE WHEEL

Also known as the sacred hoop, the medicine wheel is used to help meditation and is a symbol of Native American spiritual beliefs. It is a circle bisected by two lines, which symbolize the blue road of spirit (east to west) and the red road of life (south to north). The resulting four sections of the circle represent the seasons of the year. As with the stone circle, each cardinal point is associated with a direction of the compass, and with particular attributes that can be related to times and situations in your own life. The east is the place of inspiration and the inception of a new idea. Progressing around the wheel, the next direction is south, related to consolidation of the cycle. West is the place where the fruits of an endeavour can be harvested. The final direction is north, the place to recuperate and reflect.

The circle can be used to relate to your position in a given cycle, and to find the best course of action to take to see a natural outcome: to decide whether you should be starting something new, or to concentrate on nurturing what you have at present, accepting the gains from a situation or drawing your strength inwards.

# USING HERBS AND INCENSE

*ABOVE: An ancient Jewish priest using incense.*

When performing shamanic practices it is good to begin by preparing yourself spiritually and physically, to approach the undertaking in an open and honest manner. Purifying is a very positive act, which simultaneously cleanses the spirit and relaxes the body.

Incense has long been used in many cultures as a means of spiritual cleansing. The scent acts at a physical level, inducing a sense of calm and relaxation, while the smoke pervades the spirit, washing away the accumulated grime of negative influences that may have adhered to it. Burning a joss-stick is a familiar use of incense: you may light one simply for its pleasing effect, but when the burning is performed with conscious intent the effect is magnified.

Native Americans use several herbs in purifying ceremonies, notably sage, sweetgrass and cedar, either separately or together.

favour dry conditions but are found more widely. Sage has a transformative property, working upon negative energies that are somehow clouding an aura. It changes these negative influences to enable them to act for the benefit of the person, place or object whose aura is being cleansed.

## CEDAR

A purifying incense, cedar is very beneficial for healing on both physical and spiritual levels. The small, flat leaves can be burned alone on a hot rock – as in a sweatlodge – or on a hot coal, or they can be mixed with loose sage into a ball for burning. The sharp, sweet smoke produced is very refreshing

*ABOVE: Cedar cleanses the spirit and clears the mind.*

and calming, having an uplifting effect on the spirit and enhancing clarity of mind.

## SAGE

The term "sage" is a catch-all for the main herbs used in spiritual cleansing. Many varieties of sage and sage-like plants are used, including White Mountain sage, which grows mainly in California, and the sagebrushes and wormwoods, which also

*ABOVE: White sage transforms negative energies.*

## SWEETGRASS

Also called "Hair of the Mother", sweetgrass is a tough, fibrous plant that grows in wetland conditions. Often used to make braids, it attracts beneficial energies to the user, calling on spirits to give strength and guidance.

*ABOVE: Sweetgrass is usually braided before burning.*

## MAKING A SWEETGRASS BRAID

Making your own braid gives greater significance to its burning.

**1** Tie one end of the bundle of sweetgrass, divide into three sections and braid.

**2** Once the sweetgrass braid is lit, extinguish the flame so that the grass smoulders for a short while. Waft the braid in front of your face to inhale the smoke, and repeat four times.

## INCENSE

There are many different incenses to choose, with different aromas and properties. Frankincense has been prized for thousands of years. It is a natural tree resin which is often used as a meditation aid. Piñon is a tree resin from North America with cleansing and clarifying properties. Temple Balls are a blend of gums, herbs and oils including elemi, juniper and sandalwood. They cleanse the air, affect atmospheres and relax the body.

*ABOVE: Incense smoke affects spiritual and physical levels.*

*ABOVE: Frankincense (granules), piñon (red nodules) and temple balls are just a few of the incenses that are available.*

# SMUDGING

When you are smudging you are cleansing the aura, the energy shell of a physical body. Just as your body can become dirty, so too can your aura, and smudging can clean it. The smoke from the herbs used acts like the soap when washing, picking up the negative grime that accumulates to the aura. Following the same analogy, the wind from a smudge fan acts like the water carrying away the grime as it blows through the aura, leaving the smudgee feeling refreshed and uplifted. Visualization, altars and smudging are all ways of creating a sacred space both within and without, and are powerful aids in aligning with the natural forces of the universe.

## PERFORMING A SMUDGE

While smudging someone, focus on the cleansing action of the herbs and hold the intent of cleansing the recipient in your mind. Sense the person's energy as you work, and imagine the smoke carrying away the grubbiness as it blows through the aura. Stroking with the fan serves to preen the aura and signal the end of the ritual.

**1** Light the smudge stick and use a smudge fan or feather to fan it until it is glowing strongly and there is plenty of smoke.

**2** Your partner should stand with arms outspread, focusing on the cleansing. Fan the smoke over the body, starting at the head and finishing with the feet.

**3** When you feel the ritual is complete, finish off by stroking down the aura with the fan, ending the strokes with a flick.

## SMUDGE STICKS

Smudge sticks are densely packed bundles of herbs, often including mixtures of white sage, sweetgrass and cedar, which can be obtained from most alternative or New Age shops. When lit, they smoulder slowly and produce clouds of fragrant smoke. This smoke can be used for smudging, or just to scent a room with natural incense. When smudging, the smoke is wafted over the body using a smudge fan, or just a single feather.

*ABOVE: Smudge sticks made from cedar, sweetgrass and sage.*

## SMUDGING A PLACE

You can perform a smudging on places and objects as well as on people. The smoke from smudging will help to cleanse or purify a small area of a room or an entire building, and can also be used on an item, perhaps before using it in a ceremony. When a new home is first moved into, smudging can help clear any residual influences of the previous occupants, especially if you can perform it when the place is empty. Whenever or wherever you feel it is appropriate, smudging can be performed.

The principle is the same as that for smudging a person: cover the whole area and try to feel if there are any particular areas that need a little extra attention. You can finish off by drawing a circle in the air with the fan to close the ritual and seal the cleansing.

*ABOVE: Smudging can also be used to cleanse an area or place.*

# RITUAL

*He watched the lazy curl of smoke spiral upwards from the dying glow of the sweet-grass braid. Holding the pinch of tobacco loosely in his left hand he raised his arm aloft as he offered it to the sky and sent his thanks flying from his heart. Stooping, he pressed his hand to the ground and recognized the Mother with gratitude. In turn, the tobacco was proffered to the four directions as he thanked them for their teachings. Finally, on bended knees, he placed the offering on the small rock altar and sat back on his heels as a sense of serenity and belonging washed over him.*

We are all creatures of habit, with certain ways of performing various tasks, from cleaning our homes and ourselves to preparing food. What differentiates habit from ritual is the intent of the action. Performing an act with conscious intent has the effect of increasing the efficiency of that act. This is because the intent carries to other levels of your being. If you take a shower with the intent in mind of cleansing your spirit as well as your physical body, the overall cleansing effect is greater. In the same way, rituals help strengthen our connection with the universe. Just as vibrations spread across a spider's web or ripples radiate across water, a simple ritual can have far-reaching effects on you and those with whom you relate.

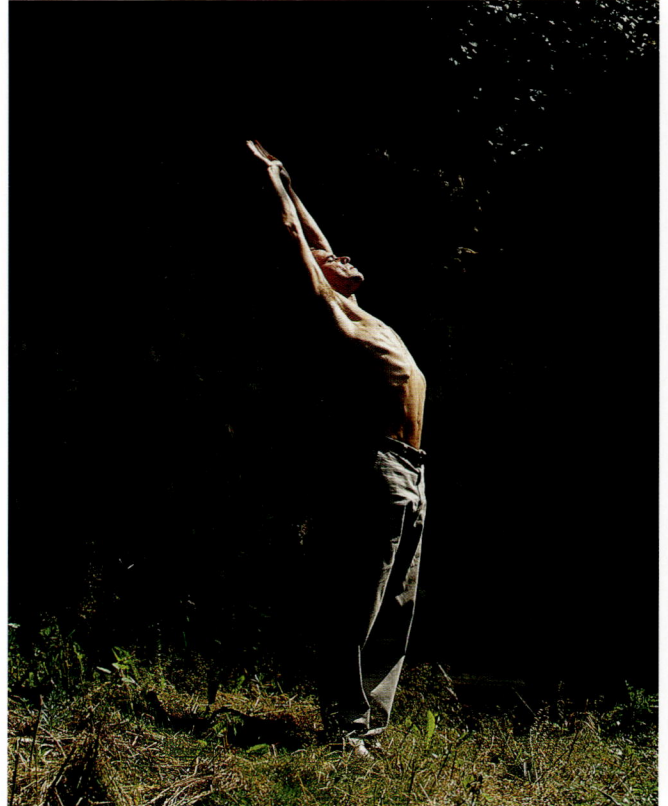

*ABOVE: Greeting the day outside has particular significance.*

## MORNING RITUAL

Greeting the morning is a great way to start a new day. Work out your own simple ritual involving a few stretches followed by a moment of quiet or meditation to collect yourself for the day. If you can be outside for your morning ritual it will have greater significance. The set of yoga moves called "Salute to the Sun" requires little time or space and the movements invigorate the body at the same time as the ritual strengthens the spiritual bond you have with creation.

## EATING AS RITUAL

Food preparation and eating are powerfully symbolic activities, and a good time to incorporate ritual with day-to-day practicality. When you are preparing food, do it with love and appreciation of what has been supplied by the beautiful Mother to give you nourishment.

It is better to eat natural foods in preference to processed ones, and organically produced food in preference to intensively farmed products. This is not only beneficial to your health but also from a spiritual point of view. Foods that have been raised without recourse to pesticides and inorganic fertilizers have more goodness and flavour and a closer connection with the Earth, therefore more of those attributes are entering your body. As you prepare food endow it with love and appreciation every step of the way, do the same when you eat it. While eating, the food nourishes the body and the ritual nourishes the spirit.

*ABOVE: Eat natural, unprocessed foods as often as possible.*

## THE BREATH OF LIFE

Deep-breathing exercises also help to awaken a sleep-fuddled mind and vitalize the body. Scoop up armfuls of energy as you breathe in. As you repeat this sequence, begin to visualize a flow of energy, so that you are both gathering it in and giving it out, returning it to its source. The fundamental characteristic of energy is movement and if it is blocked it becomes stagnant in much the same way that still water does. By giving out you are allowing room for more to come in: the more you give, the more you will receive.

**1** Stand in a relaxed posture, knees slightly flexed and arms at your sides, hands cupped loosely in front of you. Slowly take three deep breaths to centre yourself.

**2** On the fourth breath, as you inhale, circle your arms up, keeping them rounded. Now exhale, and let your arms sink slowly down with your hands, palms down, in front of you, to return to the initial position.

# MAKING AN OFFERING

When you make an offering you are exchanging energy, as well as giving thanks. Leave an offering on your altar with gratitude for the day and your life. Tobacco is often used for such a purpose as it is regarded as a sacred herb by Native Americans and is used in their ceremonies and rituals. Salt, which is regarded as sacred by Celts, is also used for offerings, and both tobacco and salt are easy to carry around. You can also leave a small coin as an offering, or natural items like a pretty shell or pebble, a single flower, or a few nuts or berries that you've gathered on a country walk. It doesn't really matter what you leave, as long as it is significant to you, and your intent is clear.

## MAKING AN OFFERING INSIDE

Your indoor altar might be permanently set up in a corner of your home that you have set aside, or it may be a very simple collection of stones, candles and incense that you assemble when needed.

Use your altar for offerings at particular times of the day or when you feel it is right to do so. A good ritual for night-time is to give thanks for the day that has passed, and to ask for dreams in the coming night to be clear and that you may remember them. Make an offering on your altar last thing at night, using incense and candles, and voice your request aloud to reinforce the intent with which you perform the ritual.

*ABOVE: An offering of tobacco on an indoor altar.*

*ABOVE: A stone left as an impromptu offering on a tree.*

## LEAVING AN OFFERING OUTSIDE

When you are taking something from the natural world such as a special stone you've found, or are simply enjoying a country walk, show your gratitude by leaving something behind

**1** To make an offering, gently hold whatever you wish to give in your hand and present it up to the sky.

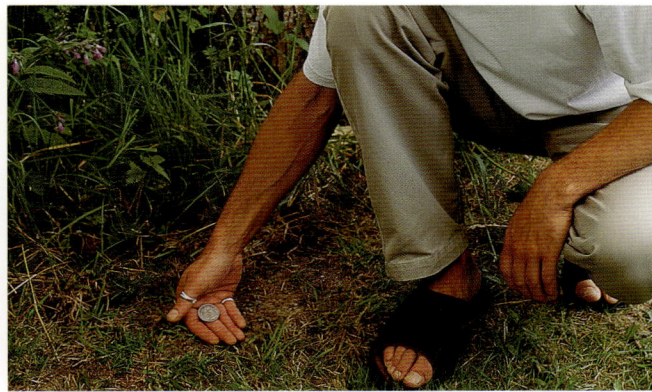

**2** Lower your hand and present your offering to the Earth to show appreciation to the Mother.

**3** Hold it out to each of the four directions, north, south, east and west, keeping in your mind the connection between all things.

**4** As you leave the offering in your chosen place, voice your thanks and intention: "I offer this in gratitude for the gifts given, in honour of creation and my part in it."

# TOOLS AND GUIDING SPIRITS

When connecting with the spirit world, shamans rely on a very small repertoire of tools to help them on their way: a drum, rattle, smudge fan and a godseye, which represents the spiral of life. Every shaman travels in the company of a powerful animal spirit guide, which usually reveals itself on the first trip. Journeys may go deep into the underworld – the traveller's own inner recesses – where personal fears and problems are confronted, or soar up into the upperworld in search of inspiration, answers and communion with other spirits. As well as pursuing self-knowledge, shamans may travel on behalf of others, especially to seek answers and healing.

# SHAMANIC TOOLS

The shaman can use a number of objects, or tools, to assist in connecting with the spirit that weaves through creation. Because we are dealing with a natural force, the most desirable objects to use are gathered from the natural world. Feathers, stones, sticks and so on are all recognized as potent allies that a shaman can utilize to help them commune with other parts of creation. Other tools, however, are those which are hand-made for a specific purpose. The most recognizable and universal of these are the drum and rattle, used by shamans from many traditions to aid in journeying and achieving a trance. Other tools that are used in modern shamanism are the smudge fan and the godseye.

## THE SHAMAN'S DRUM

The drum is a well-recognized symbol of shamanism, carrying deep primal undertones that reach into the atavistic recesses of the human soul. The heartbeat is the first sound a child hears in the darkness of the womb and the drumbeat evokes the link between mother and child. But it reaches further back and deeper in and, representative of the heartbeat of Mother Earth, it is full of vibrancy and energy.

The most desirable drum is one made by hand, using natural materials, because a well-made drum is a powerful tool, holding not only some of the energy of the materials used in its manufacture, but also some of the energy of the maker. Although it is possible to buy hand-made drums, a great deal

*ABOVE: The drum assists shamans in journeying, its beat opens gateways and carries them through to other worlds.*

*LEFT: The energy in tools and artefacts can be utilized by a shaman for various purposes.*

of satisfaction can be derived from making one yourself. Drum-making workshops are held in a number of places.

Before using a drum for a ceremony, ritual or journey, make an offering to the spirit of the drum. The spirit is made up of the essence of the animal that gave its hide, the tree that gave its wood and the maker that gave their intent. The offering is given to honour the separate units that came together to make the whole. When journeying, a drum helps to focus the traveller in entering the spirit body and in connecting with the universal energy. Research indicates that the optimum drumbeat is around 200 beats per minute (bpm), so practise your drumming until this is your automatic rhythm.

*ABOVE: Natural items can be potent shamanic tools.*

*ABOVE: A rattle of seed pods.*

## THE SHAMAN'S RATTLE

A rattle is a useful tool to signal intent to any spirit you may wish to call upon. Because of this it is a good way to open a ceremony or ritual, in addition to voicing your desire aloud. Of course it is also a good complement to any singing and chanting

that may occur. The rattle can also be used for healing purposes, to call in allies to aid with a problem or cure. A very simple rattle can be made by putting dried peas in a jar or tin but, as with the drum, you can buy one, or you may be able to find a workshop where you can learn to make one from hide mounted on a wooden handle and filled with dried beans or pebbles.

## TOOLS FROM NATURE

Everything has its own energy, and shamans can utilize this to synchronize their own energy with that of a tool. In this way a feather can assist a shaman to fly on a journey; a staff or wand cut from a certain tree can allow insights into the properties of that tree; a stone or crystal can give access to the strength and wisdom of the Earth.

*LEFT: Practise your drumming technique.*

## SMUDGE FAN

A smudge fan is a very simple tool to make and is very pleasing to use. It can be elaborate or simple, consisting of feathers mounted on a handle or just bundled together and decorated with small beads and bells. Feathers make very good smudge fans and have the advantage of holding some of the energy of the birds that gave them. For example, eagles and associated birds of prey symbolize the ability to fly high and see far; owls, with their renowned night vision, represent the ability to see inside or beyond the veil of reality; ravens and crows have a long history of occult links; turkeys symbolize abundance. You can always find feathers while out walking, so pick them up and see if they convey any sense of their properties to you.

*ABOVE: Costumes and artefacts were also important tools, as for this Mongolian shaman.*

*ABOVE: Smudge fans can be elaborate or simple.*

## MAKING A GODSEYE

A godseye is a representation of the spiral of life and the universal connection of all things. It is a weaving of bright yarn around a framework of two crossed sticks and serves as a visual reminder of the unity of the universe as well as being pleasing to the eye and simple to make. The colours are bright to influence the subconscious mind. It can be as large as you wish to make it or you could tie several small ones together to make a network. It can be decorated with feathers and beads or left as it is. The choice is yours.

**1** Tie two sticks of equal length together so that they form a cross. Starting in the top left quadrant and keeping the yarn taut but not stretched, start the weave by taking the yarn diagonally across the north–south stick down to the bottom right quadrant. Wind the yarn around the back of the north–south stick and bring it up to the top right quadrant.

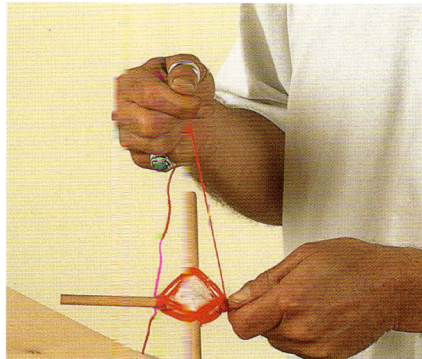

**2** Then wind the yarn around the back of the east–west stick and bring it over to the top left quadrant. Wind it around the back of the north–south stick and bring it down to the bottom left quadrant. Then wind the yarn around the back of the east–west stick, which brings you back to your starting point in the top left quadrant of the godseye.

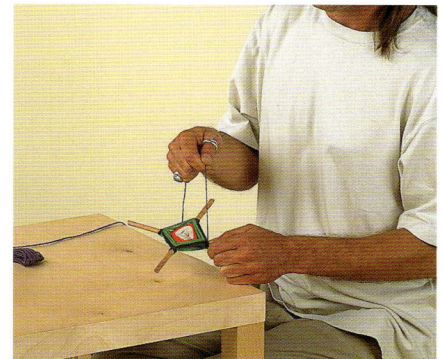

**3** Repeat the process and the godseye will expand. To change the colour, simply tie a new length of yarn to the one that you are working with. To finish off tie the last end around one of the arms of the cross.

# JOURNEYING

*She became aware of subtle harmonics
within the drum's pounding rhythm, a
cadenza that meshed with her own internal
beat. They sang just at the edge of her hearing
and pulled, enticing her in deeper; a sweet
siren-song that promised much if she would only surrender
to the power of the drum. The throbbing thunder evoked
a herd of wild horses galloping across a wide wind-swept
plain and her spirit ran with them,
riding the
tempo as it
opened a
gateway to
another realm …*

*ABOVE: Make your own drumming tape if you have no one to drum for you.*

Unique to shamanism, the practice of journeying is a very powerful way to gain insights into problems, to look for healing, to seek allies or just to relax. When you journey, you enter a different world. It is essentially one that you create and guide yourself through, although your conscious self relinquishes control to your spirit. We have already explored the concept of sacred space, and this is a good place to start a journey.

### THE ROLE OF THE DRUM

A drum is useful in journeying and it is good to have someone drum for you, as a regular rhythm of around 200 beats per minute aids the focus needed for the opening of a gateway. It is good to build up the rhythm gradually to allow the traveller to become acclimatized to the adventure.

At first it is best to journey for a set time of around five minutes. At the end of this period the drummer can initiate the return with a call-back signal – say, four one-second beats followed by some very rapid drumming. With experience, the drummer will be able to use their intuition to tell when the journey is complete. Your power animal might be able to tell you when to start the call-back.

Making a drum tape for your journeys is very useful, as you can record several sessions of various lengths and incorporate your own call-back signal.

We all have the ability to journey to different worlds, and indeed do so when we dream. As in dreams, these otherworlds are places of limitless possibilities, where information is relayed in a format the journeyer can relate to. Unlike dreams, the journey to another world is undertaken with conscious intent and with a specific goal in mind.

## PREPARING FOR A JOURNEY

When journeying to another realm, it is important to be open to whatever may happen and to anything you might meet. Trust your intuition, because what first comes to you is the right thing, whatever it may be. Just go with the flow and don't try to force anything. Remember that you have control over what you can accomplish in this otherworld that you travel to and don't be inhibited by fear. Be creative in circumventing problems and challenges that may arise.

As with physical travel in this world, if you prepare properly for a journey, things will go much more smoothly, and it will be a much more relaxing and fruitful experience. A simple ritual helps to prepare you by centring you and focusing your attention on the journey you are about to undertake.

**1** Gather your tools together and create a comfortable place where you feel relaxed and safe from disturbance. Light a candle for inner illumination and contemplate it quietly for a while.

**2** Smudge yourself, the tools and your surroundings. Make an offering to the spirit of the drum and say your intent: "I call on the spirit of the drum to assist me in this journey to meet my power animal/ find a power object/gain insight, and I make this offering in honour of you and in gratitude for your aid."

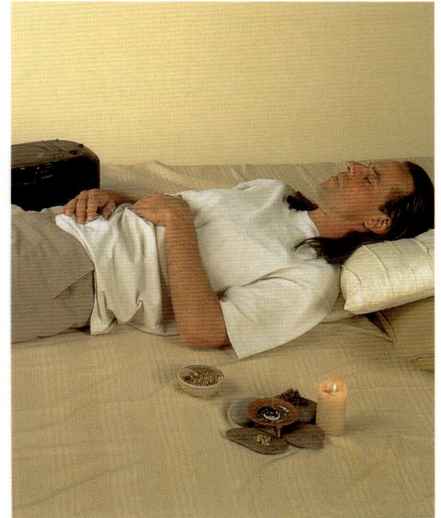

**3** When you are ready, sit or lie comfortably and breathe deeply to get relaxed. Start the tape, and compose yourself as the drumming begins, maintaining deep, regular breaths as your journey commences.

# POWER ANIMALS

A power animal is your own personal spirit ally which takes the form of an animal. It is an ally that can accompany you on future journeys and give you guidance and wisdom.

Animals have always had great significance to native peoples all over the world and throughout history. In any culture, certain animals are thought to embody traits and strengths that are relevant to the history and geography of the culture.

Because there is such a diversity of creatures and cultures, a number of animals have come to represent the same characteristics. For example, the tribes of the north-west Pacific coast of America, living at the edge of the sea, revered the orca as a holder of great strength and wisdom, whereas to the plains tribes of North America, who had never seen a killer whale, that totem was fulfilled by the bison.

Whole books have been written on the symbolism of animals. This list represents a few of the more common ones and some of their counterparts from different cultures.

Nowadays, we are familiar with animals from all over the world and you may meet a power animal that has no general cultural significance, but the important thing is what that spirit represents to you. What strengths does it convey? What does it teach you?

*ABOVE: Eagle flies high.*

**Eagle** is associated with the ability to fly high and free, without fear and with the gift of far-sightedness. The eagle symbolizes the restless male energy and the quality of seeking and striving for higher goals. Similar totems include the buzzard and the condor.

**Bear** lives fully in the summer, retreating in the winter to hibernate and renew earth connection. The bear represents the receptive female energy, having the ability to go within to seek answers. A similar totem is the badger.

*ABOVE: Bear looks within.*

*ABOVE: Wolf is independent.*

**Wolf**, fiercely loyal and true, still maintains its freedom and independence. A similar totem is the hound or dog.

**Coyote**, related to the wolf, exhibits the trust, innocence and playfulness of the child that is present in all of us. Coyote is also the trickster, and through mischief can expose pretensions and foolishness in others.

*ABOVE: Bison is the wise provider.*

**Bison** evokes the strength and wisdom of the elders, providers for and protectors of the people. Similar totems include the bull, the reindeer and the orca.

**Horse** runs like the wind and is capable of covering distance with endurance. The horse symbolizes swiftness, freedom and faithfulness. A similar totem is the elk.

**Dolphin** represents understanding and awareness and is possessed of a gentle, loving energy. Similar totems are the manatee and the deer.

**Owl** hunts by night and is able to see in the dark, flying on swift silent wings. Symbolically it represents the ability to see that which is indistinct, to pierce the veil of reality and understand hidden truths.

*ABOVE: Dolphin is aware and understanding.*

# JOURNEY TO MEET A POWER ANIMAL

Meeting a power animal is a useful journey to start with because the animal can accompany you on future adventures. This is usually the first journey people undertake. It is not a deep journey but it does expand your awareness, taking you to the edge of your sacred space, where it borders the realms of other spirits.

Once you have prepared for your journey, sit or lie comfortably and breathe deeply to relax. Enter your spirit body, go to your sacred space and orient yourself.

Begin walking. As you do so, a path will become apparent. Follow the path and go where it leads. It will take you to the boundary of your sacred space. Take your time to acclimatize yourself and observe your surroundings. Wait, because the ally will come to you.

Pay attention to the direction from which it approaches: north is in front of you, east to your right, south behind you and west to your left. Identify and connect your ally's approach with the symbolism of the directions given in "Blessing the stones".

RIGHT: The power animal will come to you.

Right: Pay attention to your environment and what direction your ally comes from.

*... The eagle swooped down from in front and landed at the edge of the cliff, regarding me with one bright, fierce eye. Turning away, it launched itself and I knew I had to follow. I ran for the lip and leapt into the void. My arms flattened and became wings and I could feel my shoulders working as I beat upwards into the blue vault higher and higher until we could see the curve of the horizon.*

The animal could be anything and it may not be what you were expecting, but when it arrives, greet it warmly, touch it and give it love. Be aware of what it feels like and feel the love it has for you. Remember, the greater the detail the more real it will seem. If it feels appropriate, transform yourself into the same animal and run, fly or swim. Above all, have some fun.

When you hear the call-back signal it is time to leave. Thank the animal for coming and tell it you look forward to future meetings. Retrace your steps and return to the familiar area of your sacred space before leaving it and coming back to awareness of this world.

When you have returned, go over the journey in your mind or, better still, write it down to help fix the details. This will aid you in future travels and make it easier to access the next time you visit.

*RIGHT: Coyote represents the innocence of childhood but is also the trickster.*

*ABOVE: Follow the path to the boundaries of your sacred space.*

59

# JOURNEYING TO OTHERWORLDS

Deeper journeys to otherworlds require going beyond your sacred space. The otherworlds that shamans journey to are many and varied and can encompass any number of features, because each is a construct of the shaman that enters it. Essentially though, otherworlds are confined to two realms and when you journey from your sacred space you can travel downwards to the underworld or upwards to the upperworld.

## THE UNDERWORLD

Most shamanic journeys involve going to the under-world, which is not comparable with the hell of Christianity and other faiths, but represents the inner recesses of the traveller. It is not a sinister place but it is a place of challenges and adventure. A shaman enters the underworld to seek solutions and understanding. The challenges you might encounter are all manifestations of your own fears and problems. By confronting them and finding solutions in the underworld you are facing them within yourself and allowing your spirit to communicate the solutions to your conscious self. Because you are journeying within yourself, you are seeking an entrance that will lead downwards and inwards. Remember, to gain entry to the underworld, you can transform yourself to any size and shape required.

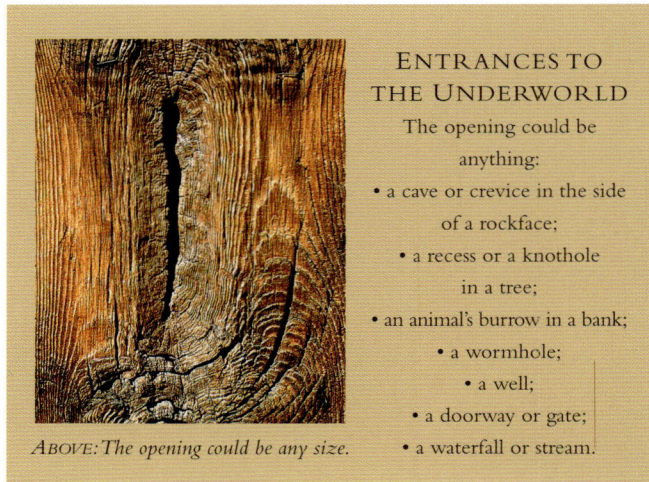

### ENTRANCES TO THE UNDERWORLD
The opening could be anything:
• a cave or crevice in the side of a rockface;
• a recess or a knothole in a tree;
• an animal's burrow in a bank;
• a wormhole;
• a well;
• a doorway or gate;
• a waterfall or stream.

*ABOVE: The opening could be any size.*

*ABOVE: A waterfall or stream may lead to an entrance.*

*ABOVE: Once you have passed through the opening, take note of your surroundings and begin to focus on detail.*

ENTRANCES TO
THE UPPERWORLD

The opening might be
• a gap in the sky which
can be reached by flying
or leaping;
• a cave mouth high up a cliff
that you need to scale;
• a tall tree to climb;
• a mountain that pierces
a cloud;
• a flight of stairs;
• a ladder.

fears that lie within yourself, the upperworld is more concerned with seeking assistance from others, by meeting other spirits on an equal basis and sharing knowledge with them.

This realm is very light and tranquil, with a feeling of limitless space that stretches away forever. Because it is related to the higher self, it is reached by going upwards. As with a journey to the underworld, it is good to have some structure to follow to help maintain your focus. Because going upwards relates to the soul, a good focus to have is to connect with your higher self. This part of your being is calm and all-knowing. It is dissociated from the emotions that have such a strong influence on the physical, and can therefore give counsel with a dispassionate objectivity that will cut to the heart of a problem.

At first it is an advantage to have some structure to a journey because it is easy to wander off course. A good goal to begin with is to go and meet another shaman, a wise person who will give you something. It could be knowledge, such as insight into a problem, or it could be an object. Accept it gratefully and give something in return. If the gift is an object take it back to your sacred space, and leave it in a safe place.

## THE UPPERWORLD

Associated with the higher self or the soul, the upperworld is the place to go to for inspiration and communion with other spirits. Whereas the underworld is about confronting

ABOVE: *The upperworld is a peaceful, tranquil place.*

# AN ACCOUNT OF A JOURNEY

We followed a path with trees on either side. They twined together overhead, growing thicker, until the tree-tunnel became a shaft sloping into the Earth, big enough to walk down. It was roughly oval and felt warm and dry. We emerged from a hole in a bank and looked around.

The bank extended to left and right and a forest of pine trees crowded thickly up against it. My ally walked forwards and I saw that he had found a path. I followed him and we snaked among the trees until we came to a small clearing. Suddenly, a giant face appeared, childlike but with curly blond hair and a beard, tilted to one side with curiosity. It looked through the trees as if through the bars of a cage and reached out a groping hand. I thought about running but

ABOVE: Help may come from any quarter.

stopped myself and waited to see what would happen. The hand scooped us up and popped us into the creature's open mouth.

We scooted down a long, dark tunnel and were ejected on to a wide, snowy plain, flanked on either side by mountains. It felt great to be running together through the snow. We reached the edge of a sheer cliff, so high that there were clouds below us. We stood looking out over an ocean and could see an island in the distance, small and green. How could we reach it?

A huge eagle swooped down and seized us. Its talons were sharp and powerful but they held us gently. Then the eagle was gone and we were gliding down on our own, heading for the island.

ABOVE: Once you have found the opening, enter without fear.

*We landed in a bustling marketplace, crowded with brightly clad people who paid us no attention whatsoever. I thought one of them must be able to answer my question (the reason for the journey) and I began to move through the crowd asking my question of people at random. Everyone ignored me and I soon began to feel frustrated and angry, until my ally grasped my arm in his teeth and pulled me towards a narrow alley. He let go and looked at me before turning and walking into the dim interior, beckoning me to follow him with a growl.*

*The brick walls of the alley became the rock walls of a canyon which led to a cave. An old man sat watching from the entrance. He stood up as we reached him and I asked the question again. He made no reply but touched his index finger to his forehead and then to my forehead. He held up a small mirror to my face and I saw a blue mark where his finger had touched me.*

*I thanked him and we moved on into the cave. When we came out we were back in my sacred space. The wolf was no longer at my side and I looked over my shoulder to see where he was. He was standing between two trees. I went back to say goodbye and he bared his teeth at me (I don't know if it was a smile or a warning) before turning and melting away into the undergrowth.*

This extract from a dream journal describes a journey, which shows (apart from what a good time you can have on a journey) that the question that was troubling the shaman's mind had assumed gigantic proportions and was literally swallowing him up. Also, the shaman had been bothering too many other people for an answer, when all he had to do was look inside. And the bared teeth at the end? That was just the wolf laughing.

ABOVE: *No obstacle is insurmountable; be creative.*

# JOURNEY TO MEET A SHAMAN

*ABOVE: The mouth of a cave can lead to the underworld.*

As with all journeys, begin by performing the preparation ritual to focus your intent. State your reasons for going and request the help you might need.

Relax with breathing, enter your spirit body and go to your sacred space. Call for, and greet, your power animal. Begin walking and, as you do, look for that opening that leads down and in, and enter the underworld. Once you have entered, be aware of your surroundings as you follow the path to the shaman.

If you are confronted by obstacles or opponents, find a way around them or through them and do not allow them to bar your passage. Be as creative as possible in getting past anything that may stand in your way. Remember, you have control over yourself and that your power animal can help you. When you meet the shaman, be respectful and loving. Whatever they give you is precious, whether it is an object or an answer to a question, and should be received by you with gratitude.

When it is time to return, retrace your steps, find the path and get back to your sacred space. Put any gifts you may have received somewhere safe and say goodbye to your ally. Leave your sacred space and come back to awareness of this world.

Record the events in a journal, because the information given may not be immediately apparent and you may wish to read through it again at a later date.

*ABOVE: Your path may not be clear but keep following it.*

# JOURNEY TO MEET YOUR HIGHER SELF

Follow the preparation ritual and state your intent for the journey. Relax by breathing deeply, enter your spirit body and go to your sacred space. Call for, and greet, your ally.

Begin walking, looking for the entrance to the upperworld, and enter. Once there, pause and take a moment to observe your surroundings. Your soul might be right there or you may have to go in search of it.

When you meet your higher self, greet it with love. It is wise beyond words and only wants what is best for the whole of you. Pose

*ABOVE AND BELOW: The way to the upperworld may be small, but once there, it is large and airy.*

any questions you may have and receive the answers gratefully. They might not be what your physical body wants to hear but they will be honest.

When it is time to return, give thanks to your higher self for the meeting and retrace your steps back to your sacred space. Say goodbye to your power animal and come back to awareness of this world.

Record the journey and any insights you may have been given to help clarify them and for future reference.

# JOURNEYING FOR OTHERS

Sometimes a shaman may be required to journey to the upperworld or under-world on behalf of someone else, for purposes of healing or to seek the answer to a question. The principle is always the same: go with a specific aim in mind and be open to what befalls you on the way to your goal. The meaning of the tests and solutions might not be imme-diately apparent, but ideas will manifest them-selves to the conscious mind and answers will come.

Journeying on behalf of another person is a mutually beneficial undertaking and can form a close bond between the people involved. Sometimes a person may be too deeply involved or traumatized to journey with clarity for them-selves. Someone else, removed from the immediacy of the situation, can be more successful in the venture, being able to see with a more objective eye.

*ABOVE: Spend some time before you start, "tuning-in" to the person you are journeying for.*

## SOUL RETRIEVAL JOURNEY

A journey to find part of a soul is a beautiful journey to undertake for someone else. As the name suggests, the pur-pose is to return a part of a person's soul or spirit to its rightful place. We are often careless with our souls, leaving a part of them with someone else or losing parts in difficult times of our lives. These lost pieces of our soul are of no use to anyone else and mean that we are less than complete – weakened in such a way that it can take a long time to recover. By restoring an errant piece of soul to where it belongs, the healing process is facilitated and the recipient becomes more resilient.

Because you are journey-ing for someone else, it is beneficial to develop an empathy with that person, so an extra step is incorporated into your preparation. Sit quietly for ten minutes hold-ing hands and feeling each other's energy, then perform the preparation ritual. Relax with breathing, enter your spirit body and go to your sacred space. Call for, and greet, your ally. You are seeking another's soul so the journey will take you upwards. Begin walking and look for the entrance.

*Right: Gradually build the drum rhythm up to 200 bpm.*

66

*ABOVE: Lost souls are located in the upperworld.*

Once in the upperworld, locate the main part of the soul and note the missing area. Is it raw like a cut or has it healed like a scar?

Begin your search for the soul-piece. It could be attached to someone else's soul, or it could be wandering alone. It might be lost and afraid or comfortable and happy where it is.

Once you have found it, talk to it. Find out what part of the soul it is and why it left or was given away. Tell it that it has a rightful place where it is needed. Be persuasive and do not leave without it. When it agrees to accompany you, guide it back to where it belongs and see it settled back in and comfortable before you leave.

Retrace your steps to your sacred space, say goodbye to your ally and come back to awareness of this world. Relate the events in detail to the person you journeyed for and, if they agree, record the experience in your journal.

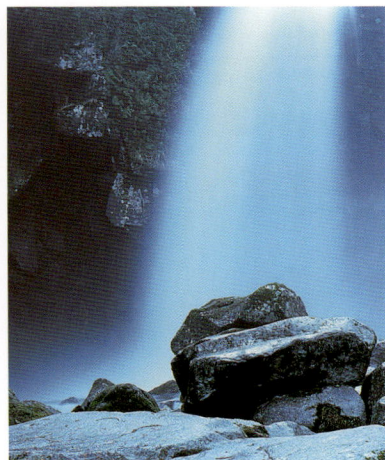

*LEFT: The soul-piece could be anywhere.*

*ABOVE: You may have to search far, but don't be discouraged.*

# JOURNEY TO FIND A POWER OBJECT

While you are making a journey, you may receive a power object, something that is for healing, inspiration or empowerment. The object itself, once found, should be brought back to your sacred space and left there, but the spirit or energy of it is brought back to this common reality and kept with you.

Of course, when you obtain the power object, you should remember to leave something in exchange, because that strengthens the link. An offering in this case works the other way around: you leave the physical offering in this world, and you take the spirit of it with you into your sacred space when you make a journey. This can be incorporated into your preparation ritual as an extra step. To find a power object perform the now familiar ritual of preparation, then make an offering to signify the grateful receipt of the object you seek, taking the spirit of the offering with you. Relax with breathing, enter your spirit body and go to your sacred space. Call for, and greet, your ally.

Power objects are found in the underworld, so look for the opening and enter. In the underworld, look for a path or let your ally guide you to the object you seek. Do not allow obstacles or opponents to hinder you on your quest. Be adaptable in circumventing problems and keep an open mind. When you find the object, receive it gratefully and leave the spirit offering.

Retrace your path back to your sacred space and put the power object in a safe place. Thank your ally and say goodbye, then return to this world. When you have received a

*A power object can be natural or man-made or a combination of the two. anticlockwise: river washed stone, eagle feather, flint arrowhead, deer antler, bear claw pendant.*

*ABOVE: Leave the object in a safe place, such as a tree's knothole.*

power object on a journey, be aware of things that may come to you here, objects that may be a physical representation of the power object that you left in your sacred space. These things may not look like the article that was given to you, but they will have a similar feel, or energy, about them. They are often gifts from other people, but they could be things you see when you are out walking, or even shopping. The key is to be aware.

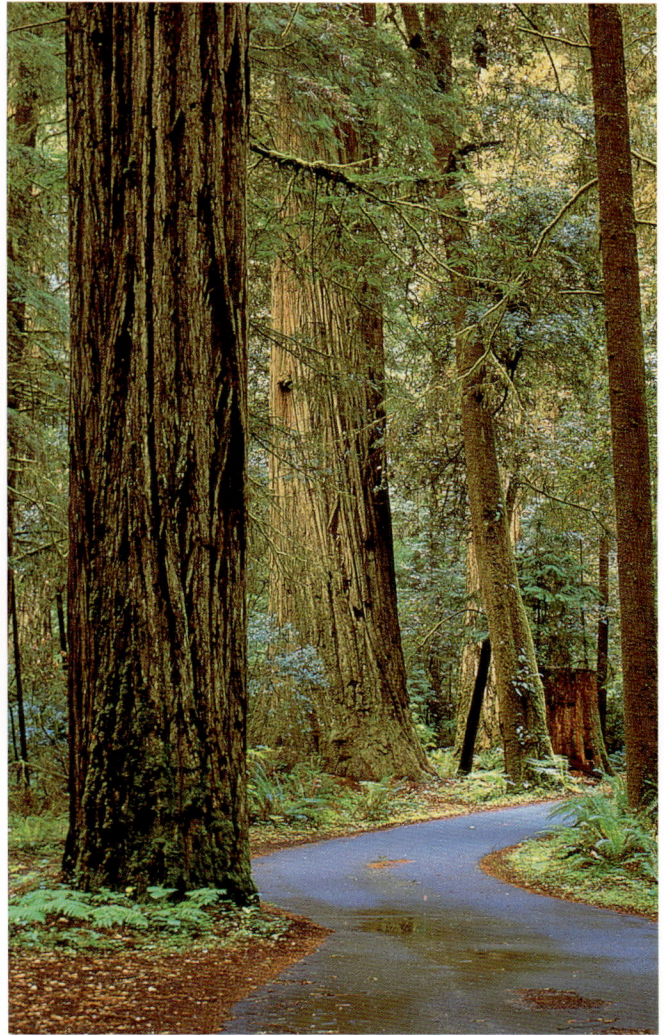

*ABOVE: The path will lead to what you seek.*

69

# RECEIVING A SYMBOL

Symbols are potent images, and it probably won't surprise you to learn that, as a shaman, you can discover or create your own symbols for personal empowerment. Returning to the idea that dreamworlds and reality are essentially the same, symbols that appear in dreams and journeys have their own reality and strength. In essence, a power animal is a symbol, as is a power object, and just as you journeyed to find an object or an ally, similar journeys can be undertaken to discover a particular symbol to aid you in healing or self-empowerment. Such a symbol could take any form: a word, a picture, a song, a design or even a person. The important thing is that it is significant to you and that it conveys a strength that you can call upon.

Any symbol that you receive on a journey or in a dream can be represented physically in this world. For example, a design or an image can be drawn; a word or phrase can be written down. These images can be displayed around your home so that you can focus your attention on them to gain the benefits they offer. A song can be sung whenever necessary for the same purpose, and a person can be represented by a drawing or even a photograph.

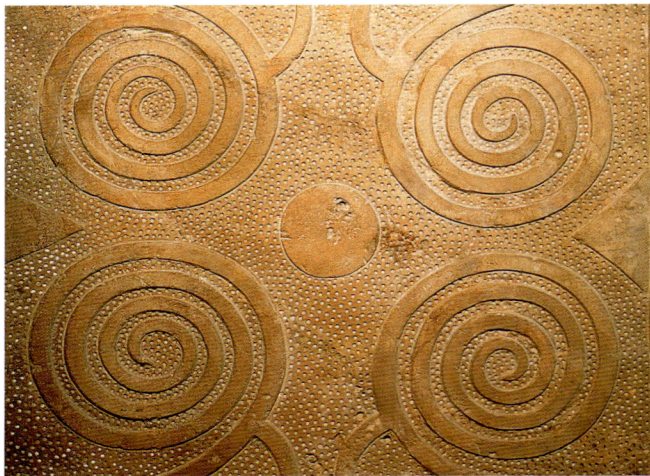

*ABOVE: The symbol you find on a journey might be inspired by an ancient symbol you have seen in this world.*

You don't need to go on a journey to create a symbol but you do need to be in a relaxed state to let your creative intuition flow freely and to contact your higher self. Whatever forms your symbols take, you need to focus your attention on them to get the maximum benefits. It is not enough just to have them lying around. If the symbol is an image, spend some time each day concentrating on it; if it is a word, phrase or song, say it aloud or read it, and if it's solid, handle it and note its detail.

70

## JOURNEY TO FIND A SYMBOL

Symbols are a form of positive visualization, so you need to focus on an area of your life where you would like to see some improvement, such as a new job or a different lifestyle. Once you have the concept in mind, perform a simple ritual to help focus your attention. Once you start receiving images or words, write them down or draw them as they come. Don't worry about fine details at this stage, because the main thing you are after is the form, and you can embellish it later. When you have finished, thank your higher self for helping you and see what you have come up with. There is no limit to the number of symbols that you can acquire or create, although if you have too many you may become a bit confused about what you are trying to achieve. As with a power object, be aware of things that come to you that may have a similar feel to them, things that may represent your symbol in this world.

**1** Light a candle for inner illumination. Make yourself comfortable as you sit and contemplate the flame for a while.

**2** Smudge yourself to cleanse and calm yourself. Smudge the tools you are using and the place where you will be sitting.

**3** Holding a pad and pencil, close your eyes and breathe deeply to relax. Keep breathing deeply and concentrate on your objective. Ask your higher self to give you a symbol that will help you to achieve your aim.

# DREAMS

# DREAMS AND DREAMING

*ABOVE:* A Midsummer Night's Dream *by Sir Joseph Noel Paton (1821–1901). In Shakespeare's play, Oberon casts a spell on Titania as she sleeps.*

By their very nature dreams are ephemeral, and very often impossible to remember. If we do remember them it is often in the form of a confused series of images and feelings, but sometimes we have a dream which is so startlingly vivid that it stays with us for hours, or even days, afterwards.

There are countless theories as to why we dream, including a few to suggest that dreams are meaningless – simply the brain's way of disposing of the debris of the day. Yet to dismiss the significance of dreams and the role they play would be to ignore a part of our experience that is not only fascinating but can also be insightful and inspiring.

We have been intrigued by dreams throughout history and across different cultures. The Ancient Egyptians and Greeks slept in temples to encourage particular dreams, and various Native American tribes performed special dream rituals. We do not have to go to that extent to get in touch with our dream world, but we can learn to remember our dreams more clearly and understand them better. This in turn could lead to a greater understanding of ourselves and the people and influences in our lives.

Dream analysis isn't straightforward. We dream in a language of symbols and images, which need to be interpreted. This can sometimes be obvious, as with

*LEFT: The dreams we have can be fanciful and impressionistic, as illustrated by* Le Chimère à L'île de Sarah Bernhardt (The chimera on the Island of Sarah Bernhardt) *by Georges Clairin (1843–1919).*

74

a dream about a supervisor at work who turns into a monster, but at other times we need to dig a little deeper to uncover a possible meaning. We must take into account what is happening in our waking life and how this relates to the dream, but some dreams may be about some inner process that has little obvious connection with other events. Once we begin to look at our dreams more closely, we may discover that themes or patterns begin to recur. We may even find that as a result of paying attention to our dreams, we dream more and remember the dreams more clearly. Every dream is unique, and the feelings of the dreamer are a crucial element in interpreting them.

Dreaming is by no means always a pleasant experience – many dreams are disturbing or even terrifying. But paying attention to these dreams can be particularly fruitful, as it can help us to understand and deal with life's problems.

Exploring dreams may reveal different aspects of ourselves, offer an interesting perspective on life, or fire our imagination and creative potential. They offer a key to a whole world of experience, which can become a lifelong adventure.

*RIGHT:* The Dream of Philip II *by El Greco (1541-1614). Philip II was said to have experienced a religious vision that inspired him in his efforts to strengthen the Catholic Church.*

# FOLLOWING DREAMS

Although we all know that a good night's sleep is essential to good health and mental well-being, our dreams are often puzzling and at times even disturbing, so it is natural for us to want to understand them. Whereas we once interpreted our dreams as omens for future events, today we are more likely to view them as a way to self-understanding. By learning how to fathom common themes and scenarios and compare these with events in our own lives, we can find out much about our own anxieties and desires. With training, some people can even influence the outcome of their dreams.

# The History and Culture of Dreams

Dreams have always held a great fascination for us. At different times, and in different cultures, they have been seen as warnings, prophecies or messages from the gods, and they have been bestowed with the power to solve problems, heal sickness and provide spiritual revelation. Shamans, priests and wise men were ancient dream therapists, revered figures in society who were relied upon to interpret dreams.

Methods of dream interpretation change, and we understand and use dreams in different ways, according to the beliefs of our society, but our desire to look for the significance in them has remained constant.

### The Egyptians

The Ancient Egyptian civilization, which dates back as far as 4000 BC, was probably the first to develop a system of dream interpretation. The Egyptians understood dreams in terms of opposites: a happy dream meant that something bad was going to happen, while a nightmare was a sign of better days ahead.

Dreams were believed to contain messages from a variety of divinities or spirits, and herbal remedies would be taken to

*ABOVE: The dream stele of Thutmose IV records a particular dream: he was ordered by the gods to free the sphinx from the sand. In return they would help him to become king.*

*ABOVE: Imhotep was closely associated with healing and dreams. When ill, the Egyptians would visit a sanctuary where the gods would tell them in a dream what they must do to be healed.*

encourage the good spirits and fend off the bad. Professional dream interpreters lived at these temples, and people would sleep there in the hope that the gods would send them a message through their dreams. This practice, known as "incubation", was widespread and is known to have existed in several ancient civilizations.

## ANCIENT GREECE

The Greeks were very interested in dreams and created a complex dream lore. They made a distinction between "true" and "false" dreams, breaking down the "true" or significant dreams into three categories:

- *the symbolic dream* – in which events appear as metaphors and cannot be understood without interpretation.

- *the vision dream* – seen as a pre-enactment of a future event.

- *the oracle dream* – in which a dream figure reveals what will or will not happen.

The Greek poet, Homer, used oracle dreams in his epic poems about the Trojan War, the Iliad and the Odyssey, both thought to have been written in the 8th century bc. In these epics, dreams often take the form of a visit from a dream figure (a god or a ghost), who appears at the head of the bed and delivers a message to the sleeper, and then usually disappears through a keyhole.

Dreams, in particular oracle dreams, were regarded as messages from the gods and were eagerly sought. Later in time, the practice of dream incubation (sleeping in temples to encourage significant dreams) was a highly organized activity. The Greeks regarded dreams as a source of healing; sick people in search of a cure would sleep at temples dedicated to Aesculapius, a magical healer-turned-god, who provided healing and medical advice in dreams.

One of the earliest dream-interpretation books was written by the Greek diviner and dream interpreter, Artemidorus, in the 2nd century AD. His five-volume work, the Oneirocritica ("The Interpretation of Dreams"), is both a dream dictionary and compilation of Greek dream lore, and includes his own observations on the subject. He was one of the first to realize the importance of taking the dreamer's personality and circumstances into account when interpreting a dream.

*RIGHT: A Greek woman asleep, 2nd century BC. The Greeks developed a complex dream lore.*

## THE BIBLE

There are countless examples of dreams in the Bible, which appear as one of the more common forms of communication with God. In Biblical times the Israelites were revered as dream interpreters by the Babylonians and Egyptians. One of the best-known was Joseph, whose story is told in the Book of Genesis. The eleventh and favourite child of Jacob, Joseph was hated by his brothers, who sold him into slavery in Egypt. There Joseph was asked by the Pharaoh to interpret two of his dreams and he accurately predicted seven years of hunger, but also recommended a plan of action that would save Egypt from famine. The Pharaoh was so impressed that he made Joseph his chief minister. Joseph was consequently honoured by his family, an event he had also foretold in a dream.

The belief that dreams were divinely inspired continued into the early centuries of Christianity, but slowly began to move away from dream interpreta-

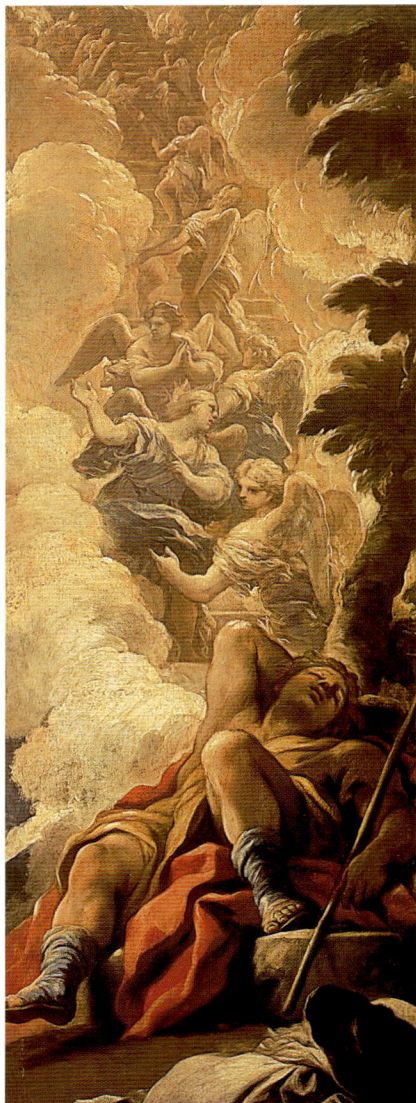

*ABOVE: The Pharaoh dreams of seven thin and seven fat cows.*

tion as direct communication and prophecy. In the New Testament, dreams were seen as straightforward messages from God to the disciples. By the Middle Ages, however, it was believed that God's messages could only be received through the Church, thus ruling out the possibility of the ordinary believer receiving divine messages directly from God.

## THE ABORIGINES

"Dreamtime" is the term used by the Australian Aborigines to describe the creation of the world by their great mythic ancestors. They believe that their ancestors (giants and animals)

*LEFT: Jacob's Dream of the Ladder by Luca Giordano, 1632–1705.*

sprang from the earth, sea and sky in the Dreamtime to create the landscape, their giant steps forming mountain ranges, rocks and sacred sites. For centuries Aborigines have followed in their footsteps, as part of a spiritual journey or seasonal tribal migration. Each feature of the landscape, from waterhole to mountain, has meaning and is marked by songs, rituals and legends, which have to be re-enacted at certain times of the year to maintain the order of the land and retain links with the ancestors. Sometimes new information on a "dreaming track" presents itself in a dream, and a new ritual is created. There is little distinction made between waking and dreaming events, and many ceremonies are adopted directly from what has been seen in visions, or in sleep, by special individuals.

There are more than 500 distinct Aboriginal tribal groups in Australia, many of which have diverse explanations of dreams. The Dieri believe that a sleeper can be visited by the spirit of a dead person. The Narrang-ga believe that the spirit can leave the body during sleep and communicate with the spirits of others, or with the spirits of the dead who wander the bush, while the Japagalk believe that if someone is ill they can be helped by the visit of a dead friend in a dream.

*ABOVE: To Aborigines, the landscape was created by Dreamtime, their name for the creation.*

*BELOW: The Aboriginal Dreamtime spirit of Snake, called "Jaragba".*

LEFT: *A Tibetan Buddhist meditating. Masters of Tibetan dream yoga believe that they can control their dreams. This form of lucid dreaming helps the yogi to realize that the waking world, as well as the dreaming world, is a creation of the mind.*

## TIBETAN BUDDHISM

Buddhism is shaped by the philosophy that the world we experience is unreal or illusory, and the goal of religious or spiritual life is to "wake up" from the illusion. One way in which this "awakening" can take place is through the practice of yoga. In its original southern Asian form, the practice encompasses a variety of exercises, both physical and spiritual, aimed at releasing the individual from the cycle of reincarnation. Although there are many different forms of Buddhism, it was Tibetan Buddhism – which was established in Tibet in 747 AD – that took the practice further by devising a form of yoga to control the dream state. This involves what is commonly known as lucid dreaming – the awareness that you are dreaming while in a dream state. Masters of Tibetan dream yoga are said to be able to pass in and out of sleep without even losing consciousness.

During sleep, the yogi (the person practising yoga) exercises control over the content and direction of their dream, and in so doing becomes aware of the fact that the dream world is transitory and can be manipulated by the power of the conscious mind. This, in turn, will help the yogi realize that the waking world, as well as the dreaming world, is a creation of the mind and therefore also illusory. It is also believed that controlling the dream state helps the yogi to determine where his or her consciousness goes after death – a major goal in schools of Tibetan Buddhism.

LEFT: *In Buddhism, the goal of religious or spiritual life is to wake up from the illusion of the world we live in.*

NATIVE NORTH AMERICANS
According to the native North Americans, dreams are the most important experience in an individual's life. The meanings of dreams vary from tribe to tribe, but generally the influence of a dream is regarded as good or bad depending on the dream's content and its effect on the dreamer.

The Navaho usually interpret a dream in terms of its influence on the individual. If, for example, a dream has indicated illness then a curing ritual will take place. Dreams are divided into good or bad, and there are rituals to deal with the causes and results of bad dreams, the most common of which is to pray at sunrise. Some dreams are believed to cause sickness and require diagnosis and treatment. Death dreams tend to have standard interpretations. If, for example, a Navaho dreams he is dead, it means that he was visiting the spirits of the dead in the next world. If he shakes hands with the dead, it means that he is going to die. According to the Navaho, good dreams come true only once in a while, but bad dreams always come true.

The Mohave believe that dreams are the basis of everything in life. Good dreams indicate good luck, and bad dreams

*ABOVE: A shaman wearing a wolf skin in George Catlin's* Illustrations of the North American Indian. *Traditionally, shamans acquire their powers by dreaming.*

mean that bad luck is around the corner. They also believe that shamans, or "medicine men", acquire their powers by dreaming and that they can enter their dreams at will. According to the Kamia of California and Mexico, dreams are better left to the young as old people risk dying during theirs.

*LEFT: The Navaho tribe believe that bad dreams always come true.*

# THE PSYCHOLOGY OF DREAMS

Scientific research has sought to reveal the process and mechanics of sleep and of dreams, rather than their meaning. Yet trying to decipher the meaning of dreams intrigues us the most.

In the past, as we have seen, people believed that dreams were brought to them by an external force and had some meaning beyond the purely personal. It wasn't until the advent of psychoanalysis at the end of the last century that our perspective changed and we understood that dreams, and their meaning, come from within the unconscious. Two of the most influential pioneers working in the field of dream analysis were Sigmund Freud and Carl Jung.

## SIGMUND FREUD
### (1856–1939)

Freud believed that dreams were manifestations

*LEFT: Sigmund Freud, whose methods of free association and interpretation of dreams formed the basic techniques of psychoanalysis.*

*ABOVE: Freud's ground-breaking work on the analysis of dreams opened the door to many seeking access to the meaning of dreams.*

of repressed desires (usually sexual in nature) dating back to early childhood, and that the best way to explore and understand them was through psychoanalysis. The basis of Freud's psychoanalytic theory was the belief that most of our adult behaviour is determined by early

84

childhood experiences, especially sexual, and that if these experiences are painful we bury them in our unconscious mind. When we sleep, this repressed material enters our conscious mind in the form of dreams. However, since these desires are often shocking or threatening, they enter the conscious mind in a disguised, symbolic form. The symbols mask the true meaning of the dream, which can only be reached once they have been interpreted and understood.

## FREE ASSOCIATION

The technique Freud used to reach this understanding and interpretation was "free association". He encouraged the patient, or dreamer, to express anything that came to mind, beginning with a symbol that had appeared in his dream. To try it, think of a symbol, then allow your mind to wander through any words that come into your head and see where the train of thought takes you, for example car – road – travel – holiday – Scotland – walks – healthy – refreshed.

Freud believed that this chain of association leads to the source of the unconscious problem or hidden meaning.

*RIGHT: The Desire and the Satisfaction by Jan Theodore Toorop (1858–1928). Much of Freud's work centred on the idea of repressed sexuality and its appearance in our dreams under different guises.*

## CARL JUNG (1875–1961)

Jung worked closely with Freud and was one of his early protégés until 1913, when their different approaches to dream analysis caused a rift between them. Like Freud, Jung believed that dreams could reveal the source of unconscious problems but he didn't believe that all dreams came from unconscious conflicts, or that the conflicts (and the symbols that represented them) were sexual. He believed that many symbols could only be interpreted and understood in relation to the dreamer's own experience, and could not be given fixed meanings. He also preferred to look at a series of dreams, rather than an individual dream, to see if a theme developed which could be important for the dreamer's personal growth.

Jung also believed that many dreams had more than a personal significance and contained symbols which, on the surface, appeared meaningless to the dreamer. These came from what he called the "collective unconscious" – a memory bank of thoughts, feelings and images shared by all humans from all cultures, which have meaning for everyone. This inherited memory bank manifests itself in universal symbols, images and stories, called "archetypes", which emerge repeatedly in fairy tales, myths, fantasies and religions and reflect our basic human desires and experiences.

For Jung, dream analysis was an invaluable tool for self-discovery and personal development rather than a method for unearthing past traumas.

## DIRECT ASSOCIATION

Jung believed that thoughts and associations should always refer directly back to the symbol. To try this for yourself, write down the symbol on a piece of paper, for example – car, hold it in your mind, then write down all the associated ideas and images that come to you, constantly referring back to the original symbol, for example wheels – engine – speed – fast – control – power.

When you have exhausted this train of thought, move on to the next symbol and make a list for that one. You will find that certain themes will recur and certain symbols will become familiar. In time, you will learn to understand your own dream language.

## FURTHER DEVELOPMENTS

There have been many developments in dream analysis since the work of Freud and Jung, but their theories on the unconscious and collective unconscious remain central to most contemporary beliefs. Most modern

*LEFT: Carl Jung worked closely with Freud until 1913, when he began to develop his own theories on dream interpretation.*

interpreters and analysts agree that dreams often represent issues or desires about which the dreamer feels in conflict, and these often appear in disguise or are hidden beneath the surface. Dream analysis can help bring to the surface anxieties and concerns the dreamer may not have fully acknowledged, and can help people to confront emotions or conflicts they may have repressed.

Perhaps we should remember that the most important technique for interpreting dreams is simply to keep an open mind. The more open we are to possible explanations of our dreams, then the more likely we are to learn something from them. Simple appreciation of a dream can be just as enjoyable as chasing an exact interpretation – and it requires less hard work!

ABOVE: Many dream analysts today believe that your dreams represent conflicts that are present in your life. Dream analysis can help you to understand these anxieties.

# WHY WE SLEEP AND DREAM

### WHY DO WE SLEEP?

We spend a third of our lives asleep, and a quarter of that sleep time dreaming. Despite the major part that sleep, and dreaming, plays in our lives, there is not as yet a conclusive theory to explain why we sleep so much. Instead, there are only possible explanations as to why sleep is important to us, both mentally and physiologically – whether we need eight hours a night or if we are able to survive on just a few. Here are just some of the explanations offered to us:

- In terms of evolution, sleep is a strategy to conserve energy and reduce food consumption.
- On a physical level, it gives the body a chance to relax, re-charge and repair any damage. Our metabolism slows down, the immune system can concentrate on fighting infection and there is an increase in the production of growth hormone, responsible not only for growth but also for the renewal and repair of body tissue.
- On a mental level, we do less well if we are deprived of sleep. If we haven't slept well for two or three nights we are likely to suffer from poor concentration, memory failure and irritability.

### SLEEP PATTERNS

Our sleep cycle is broken up into several distinct phases. Each of these is characterized by physiological activities such as eye movements and muscle tension, and the frequency of brain rhythms, or waves.

When we drop off to sleep we fall into what is known as "slow-wave" sleep, when the electrical activity of the brain slows down, together with our breathing and heart rate. Slow-wave sleep goes through four stages, with stage 1 at the earliest phase of sleep and stage 4 at the deepest, when the brainwaves are slowest. This is the time when it is most difficult to rouse someone.

After about 90 minutes of slow-wave sleep, Rapid Eye Movement (REM) sleep begins. The brainwaves speed up, blood pressure, heart and breathing rates increase, and the eyes dart around behind closed lids. REM sleep is also called "dreaming sleep", as this is

*ABOVE: Our bodies have the chance to repair themselves during a good night's sleep.*

when we have our most vivid dreams – or at least those that we remember.

We experience REM sleep at about 90-minute intervals four or five times during the course of the night, between periods of slow-wave sleep. Each phase of REM sleep becomes longer and more intense as the night continues from 15 minutes for the first phase up to 45 minutes for the last, which is often in the final hour of sleep before we wake up.

### WHEN DO WE DREAM?

It was once thought that dreams only occurred during REM sleep, but the development of scientific study in the 1950s and the increased number of sleep laboratories have enabled researchers to study dreamers and brain activity during sleep more closely. Gradually it transpired that dreams occur throughout the night during periods of non-REM sleep, although they are less vivid and usually forgotten.

In the lighter phases of sleep (stages 1 and 2), dreams resemble the fleeting images and thoughts we might experience if we were simply lying in a quiet room allowing our minds to drift. Dreams from deeper sleep (stages 3 and 4) often take the form of fragmentary sensations, feelings and thoughts rather than images.

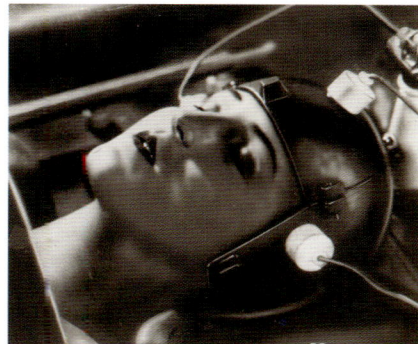

*ABOVE: Our brainwaves can be monitored during sleep.*

When people are stirred from these deeper stages of slow-wave sleep they are often groggy, confused and unable to remember what they have dreamed.

In contrast, dreams during REM sleep have characters and storylines played out in a series of vivid images. Often we wake from REM sleep fully conscious and with clear memories of our dreams.

Our bodies also respond to the different types of dream experience. During slow-wave sleep we may twitch, talk or even sleepwalk, but during REM sleep we are virtually still. Although our brains remain active, we completely lose muscle tone which leaves us virtually paralysed. This means there is no danger of us physically acting out a dream, and also explains the sense of paralysis we often experience during a nightmare.

*ABOVE: Insomnia affects us deeply. It can make us irritable and moody.*

## WHY DO WE DREAM?

The eighteenth-century physician and naturalist "Erasmus Darwin" suggested that our dreams saved us from insanity by preventing us from having hallucinations in waking life.

His theory may not be that far-fetched. Studies have shown that if people are deprived of REM sleep (and their vivid dream worlds) they tend to become irritable and lack concentration. They try to catch up on the dreams they have missed as soon as they are allowed to sleep again by dreaming more than usual, even if this means having less non-REM sleep. This suggests that dreams are in some way necessary for our mental and emotional health. Other theories as to why we dream include:

- Dreaming is a sign that the brain is "ticking over" and interpreting signals from the outside world.

- Dreams are a form of catharsis, a way of resolving emotional crises.

- Dreams are a form of wish-fulfilment. They allow us to experience and fantasize about what we can't have in our waking lives.

- Dreams are a way for the brain to sift through information it has received during the day, and to dispose of any information it no longer needs through the dreams while storing information that may be useful. According to this theory, the brain will also consider ideas and grapple with problems.

*ABOVE:* A Sleeping Beauty *by Richard Westall (1765–1836).*
*Our dream worlds can be idealized versions of our "real" life.*

## WHY DO WE FORGET OUR DREAMS?

Even though we all have periods of REM sleep, some people claim never to dream. This is because they don't remember their dreams. But if dreams are so important to us, why do we so easily forget them?

About a quarter of our sleeping time is taken up with dreaming, which works out at approximately two hours a night. That is a lot of dreaming time to remember, especially if we only recall our dreams if we wake up during them or immediately afterwards. Most of us lead busy lives, and we wake up ready to get on with the day. Taking the time to think about what we may have been dreaming of during the night would seem a luxury that we cannot afford.

Another reason is probably because dreams are difficult to remember. They are frequently chaotic, confusing and without structure, and flash incoherently from one image to the next. Our memory of them tends to be partial and imprecise. We may remember tantalizing detail while the structure slips away. It is always easier to remember dreams that are dramatic and colourful or those that have some personal significance.

*RIGHT:* The Maiden *by Gustav Klimt (1862–1918). Our most memorable dreams are colourful and dramatic.*

# PREPARING FOR SLEEP

A peaceful, uninterrupted night's sleep will help create an environment in which dreams can flourish.

Make going to bed a pleasurable ritual, a time when you can put the day behind you and concentrate on the relaxing night ahead. If you are in the habit of going to bed late, retire earlier. The natural human sleep pattern is to sleep early and wake early, so don't waste time with late-night "pottering" or watching television.

*ABOVE: A long soak in the bath can help you relax before going to bed.*

Think of your bedroom as a haven. Keep colours and lighting soft and warm, and tidy away clothes and clutter. Finally, try not to worry about the amount of sleep you are getting; our bodies usually make sure that we get all the sleep we need. However, if symptoms of insomnia persist, consult your doctor.

### RELAXATION TECHNIQUES

A long soak in a warm bath has a soothing effect on the body, and can be further enhanced by using aromatherapy oils. Essential oils come in concentrated form, so you only need to add 5–10 drops to a full bathtub (no more than two drops for children); consult your doctor if you are pregnant. Experiment until you find the oils that work for you, but the following are traditionally considered the best for sleep:

- *lavender* – helps with insomnia, tension and tiredness.

- *sandalwood* – purifying, warming and soothing.

*ABOVE: Aromatic oils can help you to sleep deeply. Candlelight will provide a relaxing atmosphere for a night-time bath.*

- *jasmine* – balancing, helps relieve stress and tiredness.

Bathing by candlelight will also make the occasion more relaxing and special.

The oils can be also effective if you use them in different ways. For example massage a few drops of lavender or camomile oil into the soles of your feet before going to bed to act as a sedative. A few drops of lavender oil sprinkled on your pillow will help to induce sleep.

Avoid caffeine drinks such as coffee and tea at least an hour before retiring as they will probably keep you awake. Instead, have a bedtime drink such as hot milk with honey, camomile tea or lemon balm (a good restorative for the nervous system).

Once in bed, unwind physically by concentrating on the different parts of the body from your toes to your head: "I relax my toes, my toes are completely relaxed. I relax my calves, my calves are completely relaxed. I relax my thighs... I relax my hands... I relax my jaw... I relax my face...". Alternatively, tense and release each group of muscles starting at your toes and moving upwards through your calves, thighs, hands, arms, bottom, stomach, neck and face, giving your mouth, eyes, cheeks and eyebrows separate attention.

## PREPARING TO DREAM

Before switching off the light, tell yourself that you will relax in body and mind, go to sleep quickly and sleep uninterrupted through to the morning. Or simply repeat to yourself, "I will remember my dreams". Say this as an affirmation – a positive and gentle way of telling yourself that you feel in control.

Just as essential oils can help us relax, certain herbs are historically thought to

ABOVE: *Dream catchers, originating from the native North Americans, can catch bad dreams.*

be conducive to dreaming. Experiment with the following herbs by putting them in a small sachet and keeping it under the pillow:

- *mugwort* – said to aid dream recall and also to induce prophetic dreams.

- *rose* – has a relaxing smell and, like mugwort, is supposed to bring prophetic dreams, especially those of a romantic nature.

- *rosemary* – useful for warding off nightmares and bringing restful sleep; also used if you want a particular question answered by your dreams.

Finally, hang a "dream-catcher" above the bed. Originating from the native North Americans, this is a net woven on a round frame and usually decorated with beads and feathers. The net is thought to catch bad dreams, which evaporate with the first rays of the morning sun, while the good dreams drift down to the sleeper below.

# DREAM DIARY

We cannot begin to understand our dreams until we begin to remember them. One of the most effective and interesting ways to achieve this is to keep a dream diary.

Begin now. Buy a notebook specifically for the purpose and keep it with a pen by your bed at all times. This means that even if you wake up in the middle of the night, you can scribble down the recollections of your dream, or dreams, immediately – while you are more likely to remember them. Of course, it would also be advisable to keep a flashlight by your bed!

When you wake up, and before you start to write, close your eyes for a few seconds and try to recapture some of the images. Most dreams are a series of images, and remembering one could trigger a sequence. If you can't recall any images, try to remember how you were feeling as this, too, could trigger a fragment of a dream.

Now start writing. You could use the left-hand page of your notebook to record the dream, and the right-hand page for notes and comments. It is essential that you write your dream diary before you do anything else, so try

*LEFT: Keeping a special notebook to jot down our dreams as soon as we awake helps us to spot patterns and recurring symbols.*

to make it a habit. The more conscious we are in our waking life, the less conscious we are of our dream world; any activity, such as having a shower or making a cup of coffee, will break that concentration and dissipate the dream. Try to include as much detail as possible, even the parts which don't seem to be relevant or don't make sense. Writing in the present tense will make the dream seem more immediate.

Once the bare bones of the dream have been recorded, you can begin to flesh them out. One approach is to look at the dream in categories, for example under the following headings:

- *significance* – is there a direct link between the dream and the day's events? Or does the dream reflect something from your past?

- *theme* – did the dream have a main theme running through it? Were you trying to escape from something? Is it a recurring dream?

- *setting* – where did the dream take place?

- *people* – make a list of the cast of characters.

- *feelings* – make a note of any emotions you experienced in the dream. Were you angry, scared, frustrated?

- *symbols* – did any objects figure prominently, for example a bird, tree or train?

- *words or phrases* – did any words or phrases in the dream seem to have particular significance?

- *other notes* – was a colour, time of day or season relevant?

Remember to leave yourself space on the page for your own analysis. Put a date to the dream, and give it a title.

The longer you keep a dream diary, the more you will be able to make associations. Do certain objects make a regular appearance? Do you have a certain type of dream in times of stress? Can you spot patterns? You will find that you begin to gain an insight into your dream world, and into some of the events that influence your life. In time, you will also become more familiar with the images of the unconscious mind and will begin to recognize and understand your own symbols.

*RIGHT: Use illustrations as well as text to bring your dream diary to life.*

## MONDAY 7

Recurring dream.

Oppressive atmosphere - stormy weather.

Strong sense of the colour purple all around.

Feeling of alienation. No familiar faces - all strangers. Looked odd.

Driving along a long, long road. Feeling that I was late for something. Kept thinking I would see my destination over the next hill, but when I got to the top there was just more road spread out beyond. Felt panicky and stressed. Kept passing people hitch-hiking but no time to pick them up. Just before I woke up I saw the sea glinting on the horizon. Felt better. Then a fish flew past the windscreen. Made me feel happy.

# ANALYZING YOUR DREAMS

Dreams are made up from our own thoughts and experiences, so our interpretation of them can only be personal and subjective. Other people can guide us through them or make suggestions, but only we have the knowledge about our life and experiences that is needed.

Once we learn how to understand and appreciate our dreams, we can use them to help us look at things in a different way, to further our self-development and, if not to solve a problem, then at least make us confront or assess it. Sadly, much of what we dream about is likely to be negative rather than positive. Happy emotions in dreams are less common and dreams are often about conflict, usually about conflicts that are currently affecting our lives. But this is not necessarily a bad thing: a dream can often make us confront a problem that we may be avoiding or refusing to acknowledge.

Although some of the content of our dreams may be familiar in many ways (they deal with people we know, in places we recognize and are about issues that concern us), the context can be entirely unfamiliar, with a muddled story presented in a series of surreal circumstances.

Most dreams exist on two levels. The surface level is made up of the people, events, sights and sounds of the dream. This will probably include fragments from the day – a person you have seen or met, or something you have been thinking about. The second, deeper level holds the meaning of the dream and what it is trying to express. However, not all dreams have meaning – they may well be just a regurgitation of images and thoughts from the day. But with time, and by keeping a dream

*ABOVE:* Christ's Troubled Sleep *from Milton's* Paradise Lost. *Illustration by William Blake (1757–1827). Sometimes a dream about conflict can help us confront a problem.*

diary, you will be able to identify your significant dreams, the ones that could be interesting or useful to look at.

## THE LANGUAGE OF DREAMS

The most indecipherable, and fascinating, aspect of dreams is the language they use to convey a message or meaning. It is in the form of metaphor and symbol which, like a foreign language, needs to be translated and interpreted.

There are a number of theories as to why the unconscious mind should want, or need, to convey information to our conscious mind in symbolic form. One is that the message is something we are not ready to hear, so if it is presented to us in an incomprehensible way we can easily dismiss it. Freud believed that symbols protect us from the underlying message, which is often so disturbing that it would wake us up and upset us if it was presented more clearly. Alternatively, the fact that the message is strange may force us to look at it more closely, and having to decipher and decode a dream could make us feel that we were "solving" a puzzle. Another theory is that we can only handle information in a limited way and that symbols and metaphors are actually an economical way in which to present the information.

Many symbols have been given common, universal meanings. These

*ABOVE: We dream in a language of symbols and metaphors that we have to decipher.*

meanings are useful as a guideline, so long as you remember that these symbols may mean something different to you. For example, fire is said to symbolize anger but you may have a phobia about fire. Drowning is said to symbolize a fear of being engulfed by an unexpressed, unconscious need, but maybe you have a fear of water, or are learning how to swim. It is often the feeling attached to the symbol, rather than the symbol itself, that is significant.

## METHODS OF ANALYSIS

Once you have started your dream diary, you will have the material at hand for analysis. The first step is to decide whether a particular dream is worth studying more closely. Is it simply throwing up an event from the day, such as a shopping excursion, which is neither interesting or useful? Or does it have some greater resonance, a feeling that stays with you or an event that seems important? One way of assessing your dream would be to look at some of the categories you have already used in your diary:

**Setting** Is it somewhere you have been to recently, or in the past? How does it make you feel? Try to think of words to describe it. For example, if you dreamt you were back at school, the words might be "young, teacher, learning, test". If you dream you are being tested, perhaps you feel pressurized when awake.

**People** Are they people you know? If so, what role do they play in your life? Or are they figures you have not met before? Again, try and think of words to describe them. For example, you may have dreamt of a child, whom you describe as "young, sweet, helpless, crying". Does this say anything about how you are feeling at the moment? Do you long to return to your childhood? Or do you feel vulnerable in your waking life?

**Feelings** How did you feel during your dream? How did you feel after it? Have you felt a lot like this recently, for example, angry, frustrated or stressed? Emotions expressed in dreams can give us clues about our emotional state when we are awake.

*ABOVE:* The Fall of Icarus *by Carlo Saraceni (1579–1620). Use myths, fairy tales and folklore to help you decipher your dreams.*

## EXPLORING SYMBOLS

The best way to try to unravel a dream is to explore and interpret the symbols within it. You will be bombarded by images, so try to select symbolic ones that seem important and leave a lasting impression. Symbols can appear in many forms and guises – not just as objects but as people, colours, numbers, or words. Some of the following may be useful in trying to decipher what your symbols mean to you:

- *using a dictionary* – looking up the definition of a word will sometimes trigger different associations.

- *using a dream dictionary* – there are plenty of dream dictionaries to choose from and they will give you some idea what your symbols mean, or could lead to other ideas. Don't take their meanings as definitive, as symbols can mean different things to different people.

- *drawing your dream* – sometimes doodling elements of a dream can give you fresh insights.

- *explaining your dream to someone* – voicing a dream can bring out different aspects, and your companion may contribute ideas of their own.

*ABOVE: Explaining your dream to a friend can clarify your thoughts – and they can add theirs.*

- *looking at myths, folklore or fairy tales* – some symbols, such as a snake, witch and dragon, are dominant in stories. Perhaps a symbol you have dreamt of has played a role in a story or myth, which may give you a new insight.

- *free association* – this was the method favoured by Freud for dream interpretation. Think of the symbol, then allow your mind to wander through any words that come into your head and see where the train of thought takes you.

- *direct association* – this was Jung's preferred method of interpretation. Jung believed that thoughts and associations should always refer directly back to the symbol. Think of a symbol then, holding it in your mind, write down all the associated ideas and images that come to you. When you have exhausted this train of thought, move on to the next symbol. You will find that certain themes recur and certain symbols become familiar. In time, you will learn to understand your own dream language.

# CONTROLLING YOUR DREAMS

There are methods to help us remember and interpret our dreams, but can we take the process one stage further and control them? The answer is that to a degree, and with time, practice and patience, we can.

## DREAM INCUBATION

This involves actively generating a desired dream and has been widely practised throughout history, particularly in ancient civilizations. Modern methods to seek a particular dream tend to be different to those practised by the Ancient Egyptians or Greeks — we cannot sleep in temples, lie on the skins of sacred animals or hide away in sacred places, nor are we likely to call on the gods to suggest cures for an illness. However, we can try to guide our dreams in a way that will help us solve problems, generate ideas, make decisions or simply have a bit of fun.

The following are a few techniques that could help you dream about a chosen subject, person, time or place.

ABOVE: Studying a photograph can help us to dream of a person or a place.

ABOVE: Looking in the mirror before sleeping could make you the subject of your dream.

## PSYCHIC SUGGESTION

Consider carefully what it is you hope to achieve from a dream, and write down what you would like to learn from it. Before going to bed, immerse yourself in the subject/person/place you wish to dream about:

• *a person* – look at photographs of that person, think about their character, try and remember times you have shared together.

• *a place* — look at photographs or objects from the place, or if you have visited it try to remember the time you spent there.

• *health* – pamper yourself with a bath, study your body in the mirror, think about it and how you might be able to look after it.

• *a relationship* – think about the other person, the times you have shared or

*ABOVE: Using a positive affirmation can help you to dream about a chosen subject, for example, a real or desired surfing holiday.*

*ABOVE: Write down your affirmation sentence. Read it to yourself at night.*

the direction in which you want the relationship to go or how you might change or improve it.

## POSITIVE AFFIRMATION

A short, upbeat sentence can help your mind work in a constructive way. It should:

• be in the present tense

• be in the first person

• include your name

• be short and easy to remember

You can use positive affirmation to decide the subject matter of your dream, for example "I, Jo, will dream tonight about surfing in Cornwall", or to help concentrate your mind on finding the solution to a particular problem. If you are using it for the latter, make

sure you focus on the positive outcome and not negatively on the problem itself, for example "I, Jo, will cope with my workload tomorrow", rather than "I, Jo, will not get stressed out and feel under pressure tomorrow".

Your affirmation sentence can be written down or spoken. Repeat it regularly during the day, and when in bed repeat it to yourself to the rhythm of your breathing.

## VISUALIZING YOUR DREAM

Visualization is a form of daydreaming, that can help bring about a desired mental state. Once you are in bed and feeling relaxed, empty your mind. Now, think as clearly as you can about the end result you wish to achieve from your dream, such as the solution to a practical problem or relationship dilemma. Now try to picture in your mind how you would behave and feel if the problem was resolved – relaxed, more confident and less anxious. Try to be as detailed as possible in your imaginings, then let your unconscious mind mull it over while you are asleep.

*ABOVE: Before going to sleep, think carefully about what it is you would like to dream.*

## DREAM MEETINGS

It is possible to have a shared dream experience with a friend or partner. This can either entail meeting in a dream or sharing the same dream, such as dreaming separately about the same event. Most people practised in the art of mutual dreaming, however, aspire to actually meet in their dreams.

First decide who you are going to meet or share a dream with. People who are emotionally close usually have the best results as they share many of their waking experiences together, which can provide them with the dream's subject matter. Use the following as a guide:

*ABOVE: If you are not sharing a bed with your potential dream partner, the telephone is always there to help!*

- Once you have decided on the night you want to share your dream, choose your mutual destination – a pleasant place, perhaps somewhere you have both been to together so that it is familiar to both of you and easier for you both to visualize.

- Visualize the scene and describe it to your dream partner, telling each other what you envisage in much detail.

- Decide to meet there at a set time. Be very specific about the arrangements and rehearse them a few times before you go to sleep.

• In the morning, tell each other about your dreams as soon as possible after waking. Dream recall is very important so that you can make accurate comparisons. Sometimes these will not be immediately obvious, for example if you both dreamt in symbols, you will need to decipher the meaning of the symbols first to see if they compare.

The most important aspect of attempting dream meetings is patience – if at first you don't succeed in making any connections, then try again. Practical considerations also play a part and it is obviously easier to discuss your dream plans and compare notes if you share the same bed as your chosen dream partner. However, there is always the telephone.

*BELOW: Mutual dreaming is where we share a dream experience with a friend, either by meeting them in a dream or sharing the same dream with them.*

## LUCID DREAMING

A lucid dream is one in which the dreamer is aware that he or she is dreaming. Experienced lucid dreamers can consciously manipulate the dream's content – they can think and reason, make decisions and act on them. Not everybody can have lucid dreams easily, but it is possible to learn.

The term "lucid dreaming" was first coined by the Dutch physician Frederik Van Eeden, who began to study his own dreams in 1896. It has only been accepted and studied relatively recently, after dream researchers discovered solid evidence that lucid dreamers not only dream vividly but are also aware that they are dreaming.

Lucid dreamers are usually alerted to the fact that they are dreaming by an illogical or inaccurate trigger, for example, bumping into someone they know who is dead, or flying from a tall building. Sometimes it can be an emotional trigger such as fear or anxiety. Nightmares often lead to a period of lucidity, that fleeting sense of relief when you realize that the horrible scenario you are experiencing is just a dream.

Is there any point in being able to dream lucidly? Tibetan Buddhists, as we have seen earlier, believe that lucid dreams are a way of preparing for the afterlife, an environment similar to the dream world. Some masters of Tibetan dream yoga are said to be able to pass in and out of sleep without even losing consciousness.

A high proportion of our ordinary dreams (some people have estimated it as high as two-thirds) have unpleasant elements. We often dream of being attacked or chased, or of falling from heights, which makes us feel scared, anxious or miserable. Lucid dreams, however, rarely focus on unpleasant events because if a dream is frightening, lucid dreamers can detach themselves with the thought, "This is only a dream".

If you are aware that you are dreaming, you could, in theory, be able to change the course of the dream's events.

ABOVE: The Dream *by Henri Rousseau. Lucid dreamers are aware that they are dreaming.*

You could decide where you wanted to go, what you wanted to do and who you wanted to meet. You could even decide to confront fears by facing the monster chasing you rather than running away from it. Or you could just decide to entertain yourself.

If you want to develop the skill of lucid dreaming, you first have to be able to recognize that you are dreaming. There are certain things you can do to help raise this awareness:

• Ask yourself the question "Am I dreaming?" during the day when you are awake and just before you go to bed. This will make the question a constant presence in your thoughts and more likely to occur to you during your dreams.

• As well as checking whether or not you are asleep, check the physical reality around you. Is there anything strange or surreal about your surroundings? Can you float above the ground? Have you shrunk in size? The idea is that you make the same checks while you are asleep, and so come to realize when events are happening in a dream.

• Try to maintain a level of mental alertness while falling asleep. Stephen LaBerge, the Director of the Lucidity Institute in California, suggests counting sheep or reciting the 12 times table. This exercise should enable you to retain your awareness during the transition between wakefulness and sleep, with the aim that at some point you will actually become aware that you are dreaming.

• Repeat a positive affirmation before you go to sleep, such as "Tonight I will be consciously aware that I am dreaming".

There is an element of control with lucid dreaming, but we are still restricted by our own expectations and limitations. We can direct the dream to a certain extent, but we cannot completely control it. For example, once we know we are dreaming, we could decide to visit a tropical island but we won't know what it is like until we get there. On the whole, dreamers have to accept the basic scenario or concept of a dream, allowing it to evolve while exercising some control over their own actions or reactions. Exerting too much control could also wake you up!

*RIGHT: A 17th-century icon painting of Saint George, the Patron Saint of England. Lucid dreaming allows us to confront fears and chase away monsters.*

# NIGHTMARES

These are the dreams we tend to remember the most. This may have something to do with the fact that we have them so often – one study estimated that one in 20 people has a nightmare at least once a week.

Our dreams are more often negative than positive, and anxiety is the most common dream emotion. Nightmares are laden with varying degrees of anxiety, from mild worry to blind panic. It is the feeling a nightmare evokes, rather than the dream itself, that upsets us and informs us that we have had an unpleasant dream experience. In extreme cases, we may even wake up with physical symptoms such as sweating or a pounding heart.

Certain physiological factors can trigger bad dreams. Eating rich food before going to bed can lead to indigestion and disturb the quality of our sleep; heavy drinkers who give up alcohol may suffer frightening dreams for a while afterwards; and certain drugs, such as beta-blockers, can increase the frequency of bad dreams. The strongest trigger, however, is psychological. If we are worried, concerned or miserable about something during the day, then these feelings will prey on our mind at night. They are reflected in common dream scenarios, which are not so much dramatic as mildly disturbing – taking a test; discovering a loved one in the arms of another; being inappropriately dressed at a social gathering, or ignored at a party; running but not moving. More dramatic common nightmares include being chased by something or somebody; trying and failing to get somewhere; exams, tests or interviews that go horribly wrong, or for which you are unprepared; experiencing or witnessing violence; being strangled or suffocated; feeling paralyzed but being unable to move or escape.

Some people go through their dream lives relatively unscathed, having very few nightmares. So why is it that some of us suffer from them more than others? Dream studies have suggested that those who are more prone to

*ABOVE: Tartini's Dream by Giuseppe Tartini (1692–1770). The artist experiences his anxieties in dream form.*

*ABOVE: Nightmares can represent your worst possible fears.*

nightmares are "thin-skinned"' – they are sensitive, apprehensive and suffer a high level of tension in their waking lives. There also appears to be a link between types of personalities and types of nightmares, for example, ambitious high-achievers are said to have more fantastic, dramatic nightmares. Women have also been found to be more prone to nightmares than men. It is perhaps not surprising that feelings of helplessness, or of being threatened, are more common in women's dreams.

*RIGHT: A detail of* Hell *from* The Garden of Earthly Delights *by Hieronymus Bosch (1450–1516). Bosch's paintings have an unnerving nightmarish quality.*

## NIGHT TERRORS

These frightening feelings are caused by a sleep transmission disorder which occurs when the brain switches over from slow-wave sleep but doesn't fully complete the process. They are not really dreams as they don't occur during REM sleep. Neither do they feature strong visual images. However, they do provoke very strong physical reactions which can be alarming as the dreamer will awake from a night terror with a scream or shout, sit up in bed and look terrified. They will not remember much about the cause of their terror – just have a fleeting image in their mind accompanied by feelings of guilt, anxiety or shame.

## HOW TO DEAL WITH NIGHTMARES

If stress and anxiety are the main causes of nightmares, it makes sense to try and reduce the stress levels in your life. Easier said than done, of course, but even practising simple relaxation techniques before going to sleep could help.

The best way to cope with dream fears is to confront them. One of the ways to do this is to think through your nightmare when you are awake, and rehearse it step by step. When it comes to the scary part – when the monster appears or an attack looms –

instead of running away, turn round and face it. Some therapists go even further and suggest that you not only stay put but actually fight back, either verbally or physically. The idea is that if you rehearse the confrontation in your waking life, you will prompt your memory so that you do the same when it happens in a dream.

Another way to confront the fear would be to re-run it over and over again, recording a description of the dream on tape or writing it down, then listening to or re-reading your account. This works on the premise that by continually confronting your fear you will eventually become familiar with it and therefore weaken its power.

Finally, you could appoint a dream guardian for protection. Think of a person or animal (it could be one you know or simply imagine), whom you could call upon to help you if you have a bad dream. Then imagine yourself back in the dream and call on your dream guardian for assistance. Tell yourself that the next time you have a bad dream your dream guardian will appear to help

*ABOVE: Try fighting back instead of running away from the monsters in your dreams.*

*ABOVE: Practicing relaxation techniques before going to sleep can help to combat nightmares by reducing the anxiety and stress in your life.*

and protect you. As you fall asleep, remind yourself that your guardian will be there if needed. This is a particularly useful and comforting technique to teach to children who suffer from nightmares.

*RIGHT: Painting by Alice Havers (1850–90). Appoint a dream guardian to call on for protection when you are having a nightmare. This technique can be especially comforting for children.*

# COMMON DREAM THEMES

Dreams and individually and uniquely ours, but there are certain themes and images common to all of us, irrespective of our background or culture, which crop up time and time again. These common themes, however, can only really be understood in the context of our own lives. A dream about falling, for example, may be an indication of feeling out of control, but to what extent will depend on what is happening in your life. The following are some of the dream themes we have probably all experienced at one time or another.

## FLYING OR FLOATING

Dreams about flying commonly bring a feeling of freedom; they are seldom frightening or unpleasant, and the dreamer often awakes with a sense of optimism. The actual process of flying is usually effortless and the body feels weightless.

One of the most common explanations of a flying dream is that it represents a desire to "fly high" and an ability to cope with life, rising above it and viewing it from an objective standpoint. It could also indicate a love of risk-taking and adventure. If you are flying in a bed or an armchair (or even on a carpet), this suggests a desire for adventure but within the confines of comfort and security.

ABOVE: Flying dreams are usually exhilarating and optimistic. They can indicate a desire for adventure.

## BEING CHASED

A dream where you are being chased suggests you are running away from a situation that is threatening or frightening, or simply in danger of dominating the rest of your life. Perhaps there are problems that you are not facing, or obligations that need to be fulfilled.

*ABOVE: Running away from a known, or unknown, adversary can mean that you are not facing up to problems in your waking life.*

This type of dream can also bring with it feelings of hopelessness and frustration because you are in a situation from which you feel you cannot escape. It may be worth looking at who is doing the chasing and what they represent. Is it a figure of authority, a father/mother figure, or something more scary and threatening? Another interpretation could be that whatever is chasing you is an aspect of yourself that you are afraid to confront.

## FALLING

Whether it is falling from a cliff, a building or a wall, falling is a common dream theme that most of us will have experienced at some point. It has a number of meanings. It may signify feeling out of control or overwhelmed by a situation, such as the loss of a job or a divorce. Falling dreams also reflect a sense of having failed or "fallen down", so maybe you have tried to reach too high in your personal or professional life and fear that you are ready for a fall. Alternatively, the fall could symbolize a fear of "letting go".

Psychologists have speculated that fearful falling dreams are rooted in early childhood, when we learn to take our first steps. Some scientists have offered an interesting physiological explanation – that our muscles relax as we fall asleep

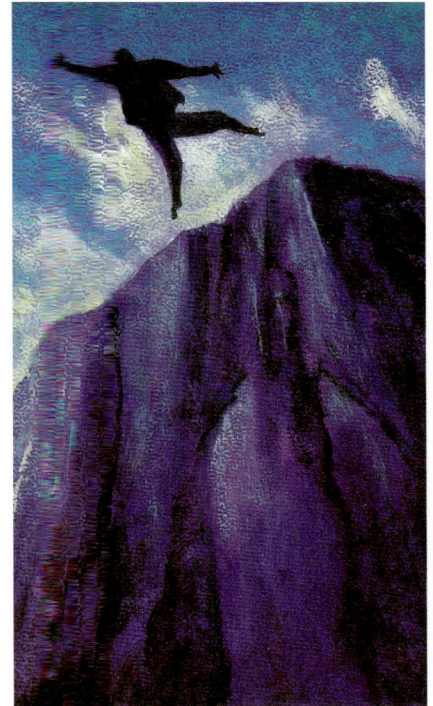

*ABOVE: Falling is a universal dream theme. It can mean a fear of "letting go" or indicate a sense of being overwhelmed.*

and the falling sensation is the result of an involuntary muscle spasm, which becomes incorporated into our dreams.

The old adage that if you hit the ground before waking up you will die can not ever be proven. Who has died during such a dream and been able to recount it?

*ABOVE: Drowning in your dream is clearly a symbol of anxiety in your waking life. But water can also represent a number of themes such as your emotions or the unconscious.*

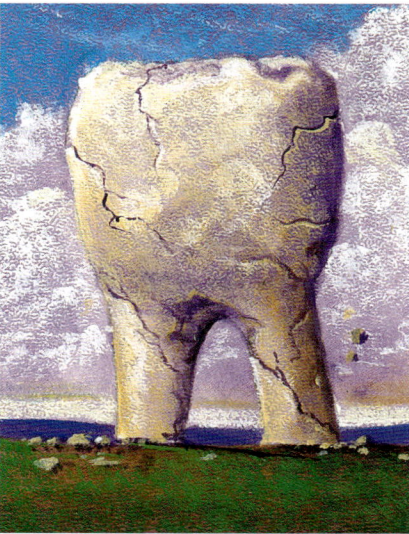

### LOSING TEETH

Whether they fall out all at once or slowly crumble, dreaming of losing teeth is very common and can be slightly alarming. Such a dream may reflect a number of deep seated fears such as a fear of ageing (and loss of sexual attractiveness), fear of losing power and control, or a fear of change. Biting or being bitten obviously symbolizes aggression!

*LEFT: A dream about losing your teeth could indicate a deep seated fear or simply mean you are worried about a trip to the dentist!*

### DROWNING

A dream about drowning could reflect an area in your life in which you are finding it difficult to "keep your head above water".

Large bodies of water are generally seen to represent the unconscious, so drowning could symbolize feeling engulfed by repressed, unconscious issues. Water is also a common symbol for the emotions, and dreams about drowning can happen during an emotional crisis or if you are feeling overwhelmed by your feelings.

*LEFT: Sometimes in our dreams, we are faced with impending danger but find it impossible to run away.*

## UNABLE TO MOVE

Being rooted to the spot but desperate to escape is a fairly classic anxiety dream. The physical paralysis could be a reflection of an emotional paralysis – perhaps you feel unable or reluctant to make changes in your life, or to make a decision, or maybe you are frustrated about a situation over which you feel you have no control.

## BEING NAKED IN PUBLIC

The meaning of nakedness in dreams depends very much on how it feels.

If you feel embarrassed, ashamed and exposed, then this may reflect problems you have with feeling shy or socially inadequate. If, however, no-one seems to notice or care, it could mean that you are happy to reveal your "real self" to others. Nakedness can also represent the desire for freedom, or freedom of expression, reverting perhaps to our childhood innocence.

Being naked in a public place with others' disapproval could indicate that we are afraid of revealing our real selves.

*LEFT: Being naked in a public place is a commonly occurring theme in our dreams. Its interpretation depends on our feelings and others' reaction.*

# DREAM ANALYSIS

Whether you are experiencing troubled dreams that haunt your waking life, have a recurring dream that you would like to dispel, or just want to explore your dreams further, then dream therapy could be helpful.

Many schools of psychoanalysis use the study of dreams as part of their practice. This involves the patient talking about their dreams as a means to explore the unconscious and the thoughts, feelings and issues contained within. The dream is then looked at in relation to the patient's life. On a less complex level, there are some therapists who work solely with dreams. If you want to develop your own interpretive powers, you can attend dream workshops, in which techniques for dream analysis are taught, and dream groups in which people bring their own dreams for working on by the group as a whole.

The following are actual dreams which have been analysed by a psychoanalyst and dream therapist. Both were sent the narrative of the dream as well as some details of the dreamer and their situation at the time of the dream.

### "FLYING TURTLES"

*At the time of her dream, Kate was 27 years old and working as an administrator. She was considering giving up her job and changing careers.*

*ABOVE: Turtles have great symbolic and mythological significance.*

Kate is in a shallow pond with lots of people. They are in a race to row around the circumference of the pond. She begins the race in a boat, which then disappears and instead she is wading around in water. She feels very detached from the others. There are turtles of all different sizes swimming in the pond. The race has finished and everyone leaves the pond and walks up a path, the surface of which is covered with more turtles. Kate treads carefully, trying to avoid stepping on them, but she can feel some of the baby turtles getting crushed under her feet. She feels guilty about hurting them. Then suddenly they begin to grow wings, and fly away.

**The analysis:** Water in dreams tends to signify the unconscious mind. Kate begins the race in a boat, which is a convenient way of travelling over water without being disturbed by it. It suggests something to do with her relationship with her unconscious, perhaps not being familiar with it, which is also indicated by the water's shallowness. The race is circular, with no beginning or end, which gives it a sense of futility and drudgery, and she is following the path of others. It is when Kate finds herself without a boat and wading through the water that she begins to feel detached from the other people.

The appearance of the turtles is a significant moment in the dream. As well as any personal significance or association they may have for Kate, turtles have a huge symbolic and mythological significance. In some cultures, they are believed to be divine. They often represent fertility and creativity, and turtles appear in numerous creation myths around the world.

Because of the creative significance of turtles, the dream is no doubt saying something about Kate's creativity, possibly a creative potential that hasn't yet been reached or realized. The turtles are also babies, so are symbolic of new life and potential. The fact that Kate walks on some of them potentially destroys the seeds of creativity, but they are not all destroyed and instead grow wings and fly away to safety, showing the potential for creative expression.

RIGHT: *Water in dreams can signify the unconscious mind.*

## "THE YELLOW DOG"

*Sally, in her late 30s, is a designer. At the time of her dream, she was working hard to meet tight deadlines.*

Sally is in a wide, tree-lined road with big, red-tiled houses set back from the street by long front gardens. There has been a flood, and a fast-flowing torrent is running down the middle of the road. Sally is being swept along by the current. She tries to grab hold of a tree trunk, and tries to cling on. There are no other people around but there is no sense of her having lost anyone. Suddenly, a yellow labrador swims along. He holds his paw out, leg outstretched, and says to her, "Hold on to me". He has communicated without speaking – she doesn't hear a voice and his mouth hasn't moved. She holds on to his paw (he is big, and strong) and he gets her to safety, but she doesn't remember how. In the next scene of the dream, she is in a bar with a group of people who she doesn't know in real life but knows in her dream. The dog is still by her side, making sure that she's safe.

**The analysis:** The setting represents affluence and stability, and could represent these aspects in Sally's life. The trees that line the wide road relate to family matters – trees are often linked to the family, hence the concept of the "family tree". The road symbolizes a direction in life. The flood and the strong current show that emotions are sweeping through any sense of stability that Sally may feel and are causing a huge

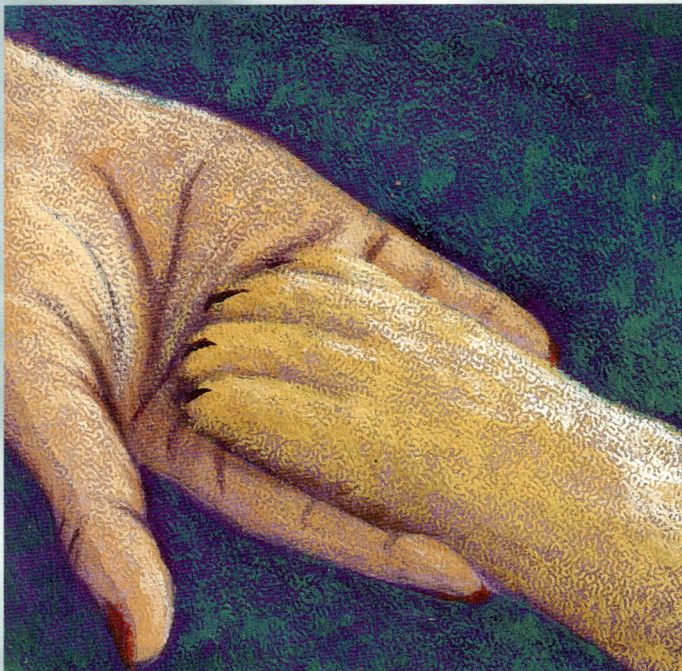

*ABOVE: A dog can represent faithfulness, loyalty, protection and rescue.*

*OPPOSITE: A flood or strong current in your dream can indicate sweeping emotions or a great upheaval in your waking life.*

upheaval. It is always better to go with the flow, rather than to try and swim against the current, but in her dream, Sally is resisting being swept away and wants to be rescued. Grabbing the tree shows that she is trying to feel grounded or "rooted".

The yellow labrador represents faithfulness and loyalty, protection and rescue. He could signify a real person and he may also represent intellect, as the colour yellow symbolizes intelligence. Perhaps Sally relies on her intellect, or rational side, to rescue her from emotional issues because she doesn't want her feelings to get in the way. Even in a social setting (a bar with people who are familiar in her dream but not actually known to her in her waking life) the dog is still there to protect her, so she feels she needs to use that part of her personality (her rational side) all the time.

# INTERPRETING DREAMS

Probably because people tend to worry about the same sorts of issues, common themes tend to occur in dreams. Sensations of flying, being chased, falling, drowning, losing teeth or being publicly humiliated can be easily explained in general terms, but also need interpreting within the context of what is happening in our individual lives. Similarly, while the common metaphors and symbols that litter our dreams may carry universal meanings, they may well have varying significance for different people. When analysing symbols and themes, it is important to also take into account the feeling and setting of the dream as a whole.

# DREAM SYMBOLS

Dreams use the language of metaphor and symbol to convey their meaning. Sometimes a symbol can be fairly straightforward, at other times it can be completely baffling. Some symbols are universal (the dove as a symbol of peace, the cross as a sign of Christ), but within the context of a dream even these mean different things to different people. The exact significance of a dream symbol is specific to each individual and his or her own experiences.

This list of symbols is intended as a springboard for your own interpretation. It is selective and by no means definitive – some symbols have just one interpretation, while others have a variety of possible meanings. Hopefully it will give guidance and spark off your own ideas and, in time, you may begin to develop your own list of dream symbols. Certain objects, people and situations may recur in your dreams and you will be able to attach your own meaning or significance to them.

The important thing to remember is that the feeling, tone and setting of a dream all have to be taken into consideration when you are exploring the possible meanings of symbols, and what they mean to you personally.

## ANIMALS

**Dog** Animals signify our natural, instinctive and "animal" self. As domestic pets, dogs have a wide variety of symbolic meanings, including loyalty and companionship, going along with "the pack" and tamed wildness.

**Cat** Cats symbolize the feminine, sexuality, power and prosperity, and have both positive and negative connotations. They can be perceived as fertile and creative, but also "catty". A witch and a black cat generally stand for evil and bad luck.

**Horse** This powerful animal represents noble actions. It generally symbolizes mankind's harnessing of the wild forces of nature. If you are riding a horse in your dream, it could indicate that you are in control of your life. It could also represent your emotional state if the horse is running away with you, or you are reining it in.

ABOVE: The horse can indicate noble actions.

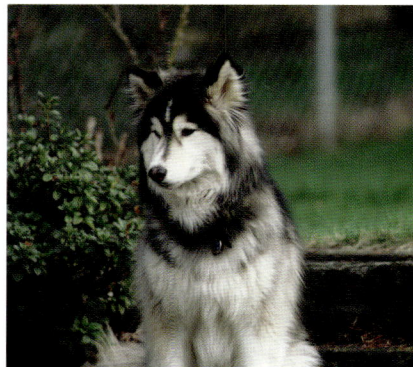

ABOVE: A dog can symbolize loyalty.

ABOVE: A cat symbolizes female allure.

**Bird** Birds are complex symbols with a variety of meanings. They fly so they often represent physical or psychological freedom. They have a variety of religious meanings as messengers of the divine or symbols of the soul, and represent the "higher self" in most cultures. Blackbirds have traditionally been considered omens of death, as have carrion birds such as crows, ravens and vultures. The dove is a symbol of peace and reconciliation.

**Fish** Large areas of water represent the unconscious, so any creature living in water can represent a message or insight from the unconscious. Fish explore the depths of the ocean and are therefore positive symbols for anyone wanting to explore their own depths.

*ABOVE: Birds are complex symbols.*

## PLACES

**Island** Finding yourself on an island in a dream may mean that you need peace and solitude. It could also suggest that you are afraid of venturing into your unconscious mind (represented by the surrounding water) and prefer to stay on firm ground.

**City** The meaning of a city depends very much on your personal associations – whether or not you are a city-dweller, and whether you enjoy or dislike the urban environment. In Jungian psychology,

*ABOVE: A city has a very personal interpretation.*

the town or city represents the community and social environment. If the city is busy and open, this could represent your relationships with other people. If it is chaotic and confused, this may symbolize how you are feeling. If you are lost in the city this may represent a loss of direction in life. A ruined city may be an indication of neglected relationships or aims in life.

*BELOW: An island suggests peace.*

*ABOVE: A fish may signify an insight or message.*

## PEOPLE AND FIGURES

**Baby** A baby may represent a new beginning, development or opportunity. It can also represent your own "inner baby", the part of you that wants to feel secure and looked after.

**Child** A child could symbolize your own "inner child", the part that needs reassurance or needs to grow up. Dreaming of children can also symbolize a desire to go back to a more innocent, less complicated time in life. Like a baby, a child can also represent the possibility of a new beginning or new attitude to life.

**Mother** Symbolically, a mother represents giving life, love and nourishment. Being the mother in a dream denotes taking care of yourself or of a significant relationship in your life. The meaning of a

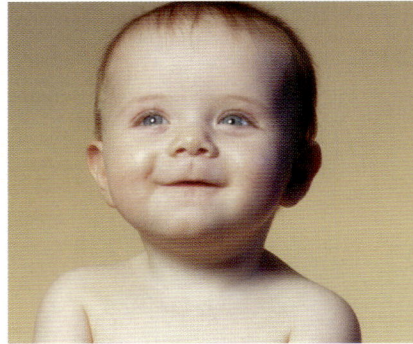

*ABOVE: A baby can represent a new beginning.*

dream about your own mother would depend entirely on your relationship with her, although the dream could be telling you something about that relationship.

**Father** The father figure represents power, authority, responsibility, caring and tradition. However, as with the mother figure,

*ABOVE: A father figure may symbolize caring or power.*

any interpretation of the appearance of your own father in a dream would depend entirely on your relationship with him.

**Stranger** In Freudian terms, meeting a stranger in a dream may symbolize meeting a part of one's own unconscious personality.

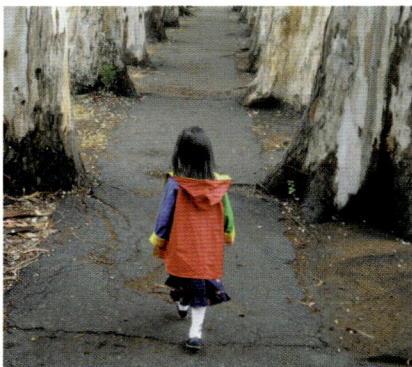

*ABOVE: A child may represent our own "inner child".*

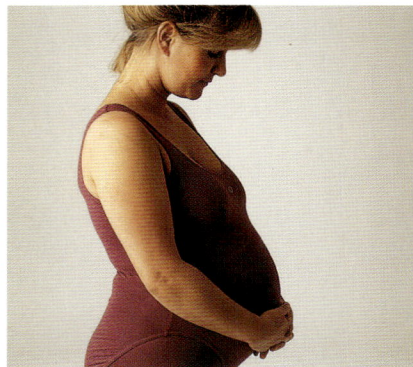

*ABOVE: A mother can symbolize the giving of life.*

*ABOVE: A stranger could be your unconscious being.*

*ABOVE: A monster may represent repressed fears.*

*ABOVE: An actor can represent your "public" self.*

*ABOVE: An angel symbolizes purity and goodness.*

**Monster** The appearance of a monster in a dream is usually caused by repressed emotions, anxieties and fears. It could also represent a part of your personality that you consider unpleasant or ugly and may try to keep hidden.

**Giant** A giant can be a friendly or scary symbol, either helpful and protective or terrifying. Because of its size, a giant could represent something large or over-whelming in the dreamer's life, a gigantic obstacle that needs to be overcome. The giant is also one of Jung's archetypes – part of the collective unconscious – and plays a large part in myth and legend.

**Actor/actress** Dreams in which you or others appear as actors tend to represent the public, rather than the private, self.

If it is an unpleasant dream about acting, it could refer to a situation or situations in which you feel forced to "put on an act" rather than being yourself.

**Angel** Traditionally seen as messengers of God, angels symbolize purity and good-ness. They are also thought of as protectors and guides.

*ABOVE: A giant can indicate a huge obstacle that needs to be overcome.*

ABOVE: *A house represents the dreamer.*

ABOVE: *Going back to school can symbolize nostalgia.*

ABOVE: *An opening can mean new opportunities.*

## HOUSES AND BUILDINGS

**House** A house is usually interpreted as representing the dreamer, with each room and floor representing a different aspect of the personality or mind. The living rooms represent the everyday, conscious life, the attic represents the higher, spiritual self, and the cellar represents the unconscious. The state of the house is also relevant. Is it dark and cramped, or light and airy? Does it need tidying? Do you get lost in it? Is it undergoing construction? Perhaps it is being decorated.

**School** A classroom typically represents learning but it can also represent competition or public esteem. Dreaming about being back in the classroom can indicate feelings of inadequacy, especially if the dream centres around unpleasant early school experiences. School can also symbolize nostalgia, expressing a desire to relive a feeling of ambition or joy from an earlier stage in your life.

RIGHT: *An office may indicate professional standing.*

**Office** If you dream about your own office, it may be an indication that you are bringing work home with you. An office can also symbolize authority or your position in the world.

**Opening/doorway** The meaning of a door or doorway depends entirely on how it appears in the dream. An open door could represent a new opportunity or phase in life, and going through the door would be to grasp that opportunity. Too many doors could suggest that a choice needs to be made. If the door is locked, it may indicate that something is being repressed or hidden

**Prison** A prison can be a sign that some part of you is being repressed and stifled, and needs to be released. Alternatively, it may be a sign that the dreamer needs to lock up certain actions or behaviour.

**Tower** A tower could be a symbol of caution and vigilance (a watchtower) or imprisonment (a guard tower). It could also be an ivory tower, representing arrogance and aloofness.

**Hospital** A hospital is a place for healing and getting back into the flow of life. It could also suggest that you may need to pay some attention to your health.

*ABOVE: A prison may show that you feel stifled.*

*ABOVE: A tower could be a symbol of vigilance.*

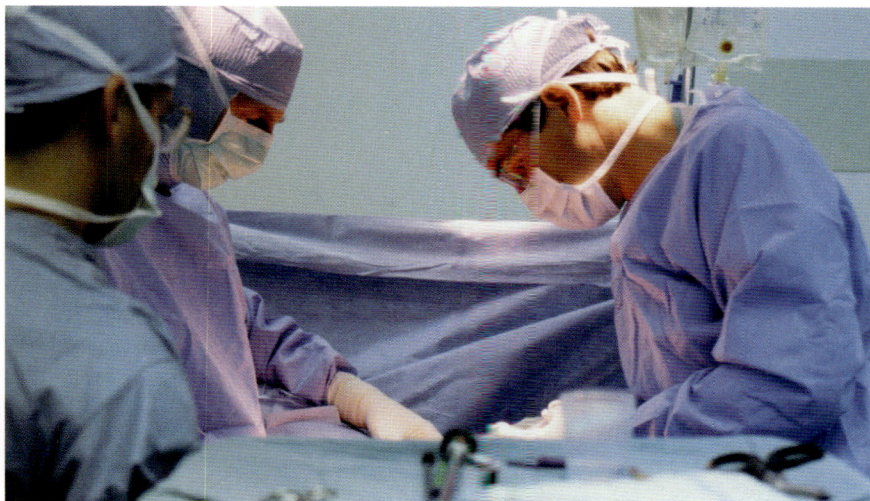

*ABOVE: A hospital may mean you feel unhealthy.*

## TRAVEL

**Station/airport** Railway stations and airports represent many possibilities – a new venture or idea ready to "take off", apprehension or excitement about the future, or a transition in life. They can be confusing places, so their appearance in a dream may show that you need to sort through a particular problem or conflict.

**Train** A missed train could symbolize missed opportunities in life, as could being on the wrong train or missing a stop. Travelling smoothly down the track may mean staying "on track" in life. According to Freudian interpretation, the train represents the penis, and entering the tunnel (the vagina) represents sexual intercourse.

**Car** A car usually represents yourself and, in particular, whether or not you feel in control of your life. If you are "in the

*ABOVE: A railway station may mean a new venture.*

driver's seat", this may symbolize that you are taking charge of your life. If someone else is driving, it may show that you feel over-dependent on others, or are allowing others to control your life.

**Road** In dreams, roads represent a direction or goal in life. If the road is straight and narrow, you may be on the right path. If it is winding or bumpy, your plans

*ABOVE: Roads symbolize a direction in life.*

may be vague or have changed unexpectedly. If you never get to your destination, something could be preventing you from reaching your goal.

**Aeroplane** An aeroplane can be a positive symbol of liberation and freedom, particularly if you are the pilot and are able to "rise above" a situation or soar to new heights.

*ABOVE: A train journey may mean you're "on track".*

*ABOVE: Driving a car may show you feel in control.*

*ABOVE: A flight can symbolize liberation.*

## BIRTH, MARRIAGE AND DEATH

**Birth** Birth can symbolize the beginning (actual or potential) of a new idea or project, or a sense of beginning a new stage in your life. Pregnant women often dream of difficult or strange births (for example, giving birth to kittens) which reflects their anxiety about childbirth.

**Wedding/marriage** Dreams of weddings or marriage can symbolize the union of opposite yet complementary parts of yourself, the most obvious being the union of the masculine and feminine parts of your personality.

**Bride/bridegroom** In Jungian psychology, dream images of a bride or bridegroom may represent the anima (feminine personality traits repressed in the male unconscious) in men, and the animus (masculine personality traits

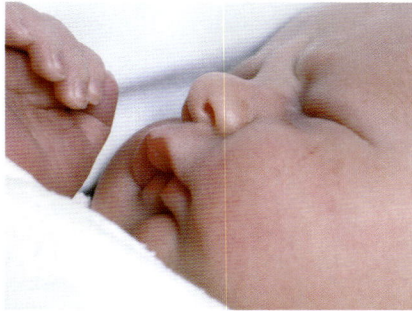

*ABOVE: Giving birth may symbolize a new beginning.*

repressed in the female unconscious) in women. Brides also traditionally symbolize purity and innocence.

**Sex** This is a complex area with a broad range of possible meanings that depend on the individual. Generally, seeing others having sex in a dream or having sex yourself could be simply an expression of sexual desire, a release of sexual

tension, a desire to bond, or an indication of repressed desires for physical and emotional love. Dreaming about sex with someone "inappropriate", or a person from your past, does not necessarily mean you harbour secret desires – your memory of them may have been triggered, or you may have come into contact with them recently.

**Death** Dreams about death or dying are not usually seen literally as omens of death, although they could express some anxiety about dying. Symbolically, death represents not so much an ending as a new beginning, so to dream of your own death could mean that you are preparing to start something new and are letting go of the old. If you dream of the death of a loved one, you may be rehearsing the actual event and unconsciously preparing yourself for bereavement.

*ABOVE: Masculine and feminine combine in marriage.*

*ABOVE: Sex in dreams is a complex area.*

*ABOVE: Death in dreams is not usually a bad sign.*

## AGGRESSION AND VIOLENCE

**Accident** Being involved in an accident or crash in a dream could be a straight-forward fear of being physically harmed. It may also suggest that you are in a state of anxiety, or even fear, that you are heading for an emotional "crash" or collision. If the general feeling of the dream is positive, although violent, it could symbolize a part of your life that you are letting go.

**Violence towards others** Horrifying scenes of violence or destruction may represent an overwhelming fear of the loss of your sense of power and control. If you are the one being violent, this

*ABOVE: Accidents may show a fear of being harmed.*

could represent a struggle for self-assertion, or be an expression of a deep-rooted anger and resentment against some unwanted aspects of your life. Murder is a symbol of aggression and repressed rage at either the self or others. If the experience of violence leaves you feeling strangely neutral, as can sometimes happen in this kind of dream, physical violence could be a metaphor for another kind of conflict, maybe of opinions or ideas.

**Violence towards oneself** Directed at you (rather than inflicted by you), violence often represents a sense of guilt and a desire for self-punishment. It is also an indication that you are feeling vulnerable and battered by the outside world. Being a victim in a dream, or seeing another person being victimized, may represent a situation about which you feel helpless.

*ABOVE: If you are violent towards others it can mean a desire for self-assertion.*

*ABOVE: Violence towards oneself can mean you are feeling helpless.*

*ABOVE: Examinations can stand for success or failure.*

*ABOVE: A bed may show a desire for escape.*

**Mirror** A classic identity crisis cream is one in which you look into a mirror and see someone else's face. The face reflected may give you a clue to the nature of the identity problem. A cracked or clouded mirror reflects the distorted face (or image) you may be presenting to the world.

## ANXIOUS SITUATIONS

**Tests and exams** In dreams, tests can stand for success or a fear of failure in your personal or professional life. Taking a test for which you have not prepared is a classic fear-of-failure dream. Passing an exam or test could be a metaphor for having succeeded in something.

**Interviews** Having an interview can show anxiety. The people on the interview panel could represent aspects of the dreamer's self image – perhaps dissatisfaction or judgement.

*ABOVE: Interviews are common anxiety dreams.*

## OBJECTS

**Bed** A bed can be a symbol of security, warmth and comfort, maybe even of escaping from the outside world. If a bed appears in a dream about marriage or a relationship, then the state of the bed could be seen as representing the state of the relationship.

**Book** Books represent knowledge and wisdom, or the historical record of the dreamer's life. A dusty old book could symbolize forgotten or neglected knowledge, or an earlier "chapter" of your life. The opening and closing of a book may represent the relevant "chapter" of your life.

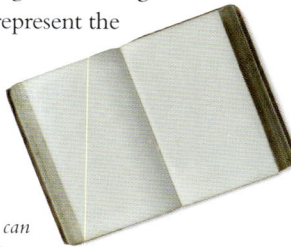

*RIGHT: Books can symbolize wisdom.*

**Clock / watch** In dreams, clocks often reflect anxiety about not being on top of things or being behind schedule. They may also symbolize your emotions.

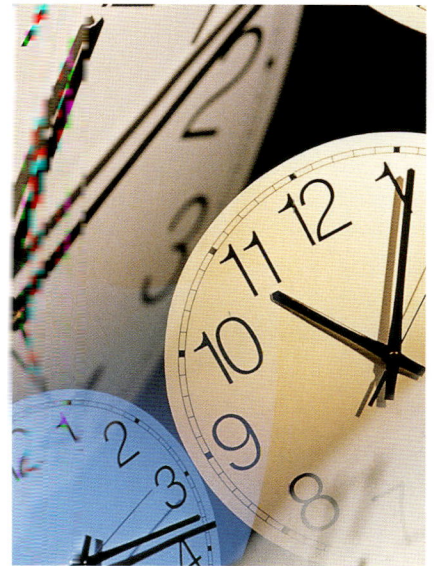

*ABOVE Clocks can reflect anxieties.*

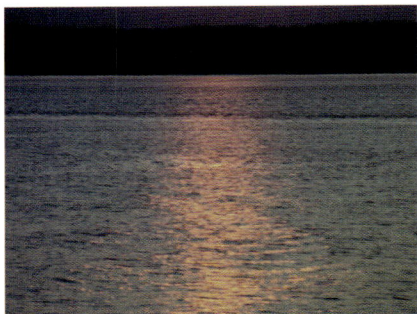

*ABOVE: A body of water represents the unconscious.*

*ABOVE: The pace of a river's flow may be significant.*

*ABOVE: Fire can mean passion or danger.*

## NATURE AND THE ELEMENTS

**Sea** Large bodies of water generally represent the unconscious and the emotions within it, so feelings about the sea in a dream could indicate your emotional state. Are you feeling lost in a small boat, or safe and protected in a large one? Is the water calm or are you feeling overwhelmed by huge waves? Are you afraid of monsters that lurk in the dark waters? Because the sea can mean all of these things, it is particularly important to take note of the emotional atmosphere of the dream.

**River** As with the sea, a river is a large body of water and generally represents an emotional state. Watching a river flow passively may indicate that life is passing you by without enough direction. If the river is bursting its banks and over-flowing, this may reflect a feeling of being out of control. Crossing a river by a bridge may symbolize that you are undergoing a change in life, or it may mean that you are avoiding a flood of passion by observing the water from a safe position.

**Fire** This element is a complex symbol which has many different meanings, including passion, anger, illumination and danger. Fire can purge as well as consume, purify as well as destroy. An out-of-control fire could be a sign of unbridled passion or ambition.

*LEFT: A mountain is usually positive.*

*ABOVE: The flower is a symbol of fragility.*

*ABOVE: A steep slope may show a lack of progress.*

*ABOVE: An avalanche shows we are overwhelmed.*

**Flower** The flower in your dreams is a natural symbol of beauty, fragility and harmlessness. It can also symbolize the attraction of bees to nectar. In Asian yoga teachings, flowers represent the psychic centres or "chakras" on which to focus meditation practice.

**Mountain** Climbing a mountain and reaching the top could be a positive symbol that you are achieving your goals. Surveying the landscape from the top of a mountain could represent looking at life objectively, or assessing it without any emotional attachment. Descending a mountain could mean that you are letting go of insurmountable issues.

**Slope** Trying to ascend a slippery slope is a common dream which suggests that you are failing to progress in a certain area of your waking life. Stumbling or slipping down the slope may signify that you are forcing yourself to do things which go against your nature.

**Forest** Commonly an element of fairy tales and legends, a forest is a symbol of the unconscious, so venturing into a forest can be seen as an exploration of the unconscious mind. A forest can also represent a refuge from the demands of everyday life.

**Avalanche** An avalanche signifies being overwhelmed or fearing disaster. It may also symbolize "frozen" emotions that should be expressed or experienced.

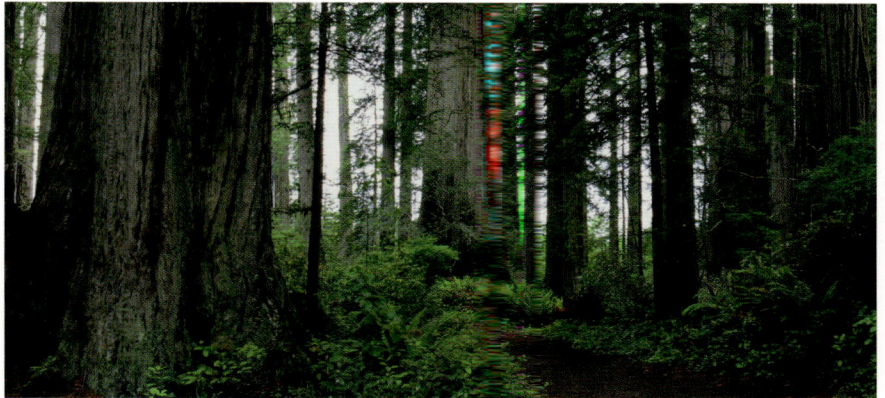

*ABOVE: A forest is a classic part of fairy tales and myths and symbolizes the unconscious.*

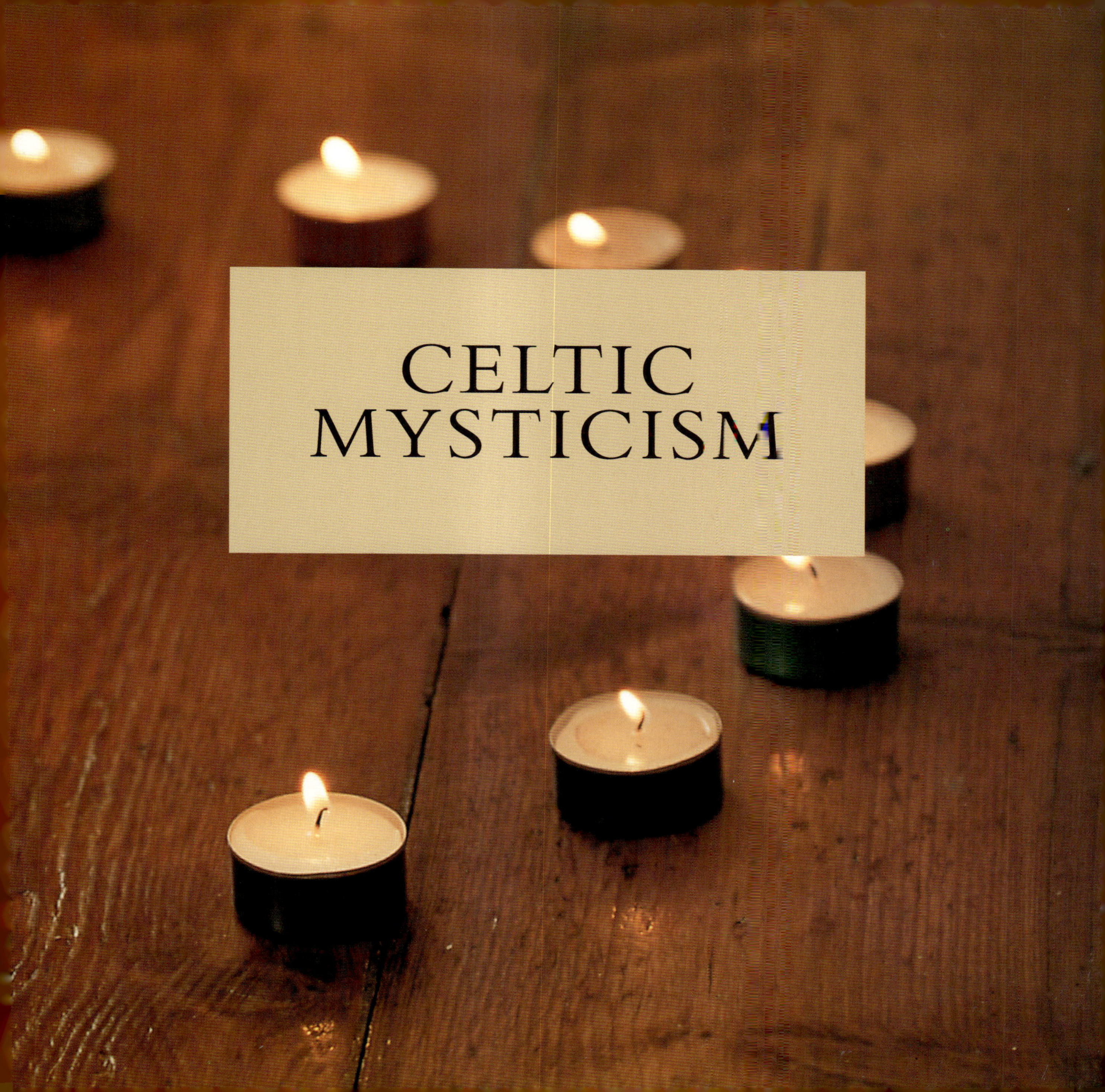

# CELTIC MYSTICISM

# THE CELTS

*The Celtic approach to life is a holistic one, acknowledging the cyclic nature of*
*existence and making no false distinctions between the sacred and the secular.*
*The whole of creation is the transfigured image of its creator, and earth and heaven,*
*or the physical and the spiritual, are parts of a unity.*

Today, people of Celtic descent in Europe are concentrated on its western shores. They live chiefly in Brittany, Cornwall, Wales, Scotland, the Isle of Man and Ireland. However, the Celts dominated much of Western Europe for some fifteen hundred years before Christ. They occupied an area that stretched from the Black Sea, along the length of the Danube basin and into both France and Spain. Their origins lie in the late Bronze Age but they are essentially an Iron Age people and were known to their neighbours, the Greeks, as Keltoi, and to the Romans as Celtae or Galli. Celts also ventured as far as Asia Minor and these people, called the Galatae (or Galatians), are referred to in the New Testament.

Celtic culture was heroic and tribal. They were formidable warriors and expert charioteers. The Celts also excelled in metallurgy and their artistic skills were lavished on ornaments, brooches, decorations for horse-harnesses, weapons and shields and what we would now recognize as luxury goods. They were vigorous traders and their tribal society was evidently advanced, but they left no first-hand written records. The ancient Celts relied on oral accounts and trained memories to pass on their history. Their myths and legends were eventually written down by Celtic Christian monks from the fifth century onwards, when the old Celtic civilization was nearing its end.

*ABOVE: Celtic brooch. 5th century BC.*

*BELOW: Celtic helmet fashioned in bronze, iron, enamel and gold. 4th century BC.*

*BELOW: The Tara brooch; 8th century.*

*RIGHT: Ballinskelligs Bay, Co Kerry, Ireland.*

## WHO WERE THE CELTS?

The Celts migrated westwards into Britain during the first millennium BC, probably intermarrying with earlier inhabitants. The whole of present-day England and Wales was peopled by what are known as Brythonic-speaking Celts, the language from which Welsh, Cornish and Breton derive. A completely different branch of the Celtic race invaded Ireland, from Spain, in about the fourth century BC, displacing the earlier inhabitants by war or by intermarriage. These were Gaelic speakers, from whose language Irish, Scots Gaelic and Manx derive.

Until the rise of Roman power, the Celts were a force to be reckoned with and Rome itself had been sacked by them in 385BC. This was not to last and Julius Caesar gained victory between 59 and 48BC over the Celtic tribes living in Gaul (present-day France). Although many Celts were incorporated into the Roman empire, their religion and mythology survived largely intact until Rome adopted Christianity in the fourth century AD.

Perhaps the most unique aspect of the Celtic inheritance is their mystic approach to life. At the centre of a Celt's spirituality was an attitude that saw no separation between the gods and man, or between this world and the next, or between the past and the present. An illustration of this ability to fuse diverse elements is the way the Celts adopted a version of the Christian faith, that was uniquely holistic and which grew organically from what had gone before. This holistic approach is one that holds more resonance today than ever before and is an integral part of what we refer to as Celtic mysticism.

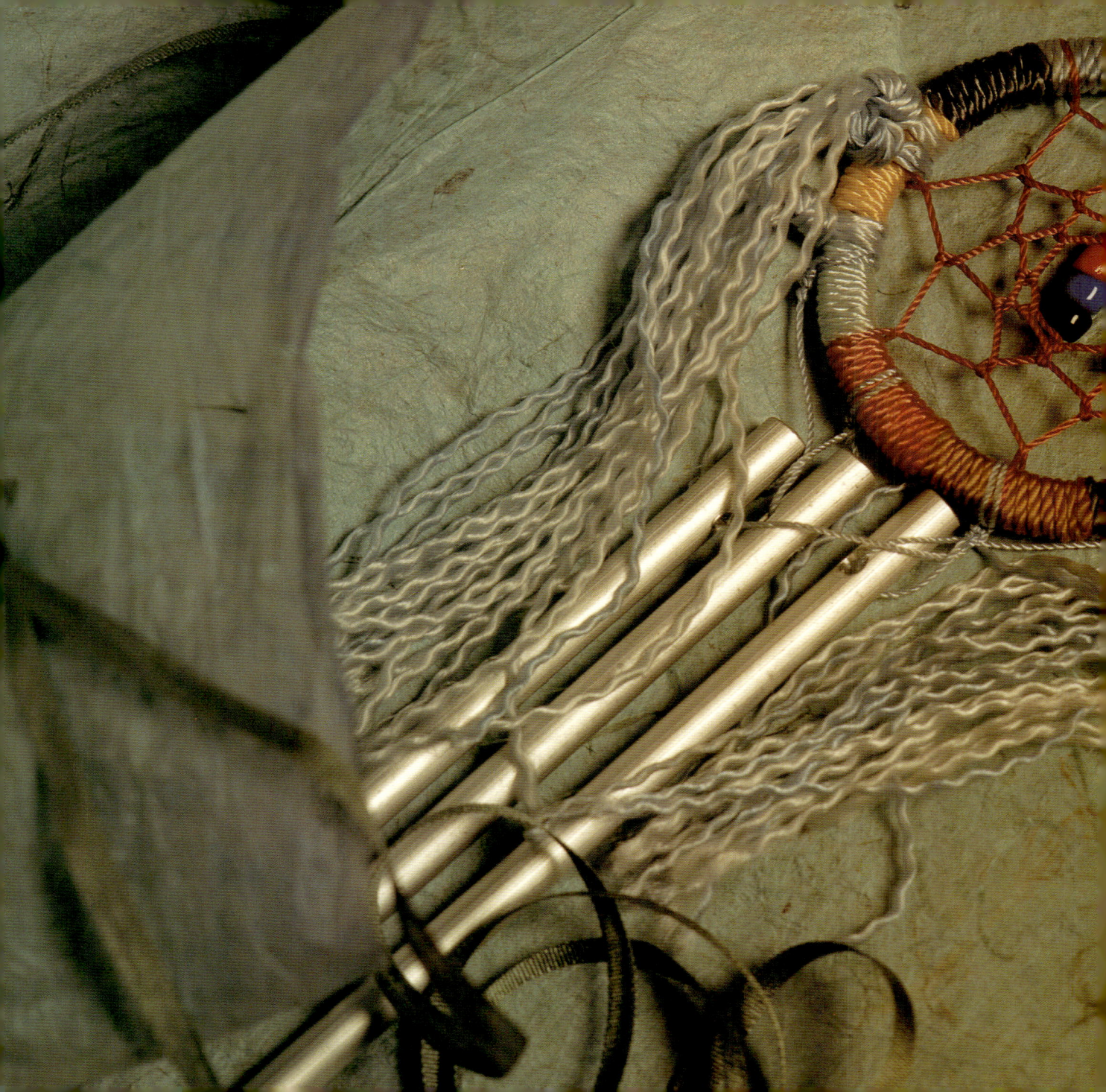

# THE CELTIC WAY

The spiritual and material worlds were interconnected in the Celtic worldview. In the past, the Druids, or seers, who had intimate knowledge of the natural world, were the keepers of wisdom, while the bards and poets, who took their inspiration directly from nature, kept the rich heritage of myths, legends and traditions alive. Great emphasis was put on the insights that could be gained by visiting the Otherworld, which is accessed via gateways as you undertake a spirit flight or journey of the soul. Other ways to gain insight are to locate your inner silence or even to meet up with one of the archetypal characters from the myths.

# THE OTHERWORLD

*The spiritual world of pagan Celtic understanding is very much earthbound. It is the home*
*of a pantheon of archetypes – and the embodiments of basic human dynamics – in which*
*the traditions of earlier cultures were probably assimilated. The Otherworld is not a dismal*
*abode of the dead but a glittering world, close to – and acting upon – reality.*

### EARTH, STARS AND ANNWN

Ancient peoples, worldwide, were aware of the procession of the equinoxes, whereby the Earth's axis gradually shifts from one constellation to another. At about the time of the Celtic occupation of Britain, this alignment was in the process of change from the constellation of Draco, the Dragon, to that

of Ursa Minor, the Little Bear. The Earth's axis extended to the heavenly Pole Star so that its influence penetrated the Goddess, Mother Earth herself. The Pole star in Draco was Alpha Draconis. In Ursa Minor it was Polaris. It was believed then that the ruling constellation was reflected in the deeds of men and women and in the earliest sources of the Arthurian myths, Arthur's name is derived from the Welsh Arth, meaning "Bear". His mythological father was Uther Pendraig (Pendragon, "chief of the dragon"). In Celtic mythology, the Bear therefore succeeded the Dragon.

### ANNWN, THE CELTIC HEAVEN

In Celtic mythology heaven was not merely a place that the dead inhabited. Their heaven, called Annwn, in the Celtic world-view, is a reality that is experienced by the sensitive. It has doors and gateways to this world, through which seers and bards can pass on spirit-flights or journeys of the soul. Intrepid heroes may find such gateways, which are often through water,

*LEFT: Arthur receives the sword Excalibur from the Lady of the Lake, a goddess from the Otherworld.*

ABOVE: *The bean-sidhe, the fairy woman.*

RIGHT: *At his time of death Arthur is taken, by water, out of this world and into another.*

across narrow bridges or beneath mounds. On the eve of Samhain, 31 October, the festival of the dead, the gateways to the Otherworld are said to open. One of the most potent places in Celtic mythology is Llyn Tegid, or Lake Bala, in Wales. There, gods and goddesses dwell underwater, or on an invisible island. It was from the Lady of the Lake that Arthur received his sword. She was said to be the foster-mother of Launcelot of the Lake. She named and armed him and he walked to dry land on a sword blade.

There are many stories of those who entered the Otherworld to find it a paradise where time and space do strange things. Nera spent three days with the *sidhe* (or fairies) and returned to find that no time had passed. The little fairy mound contained a vast community, with dwellings and lands. Bran Mac Feba returned from his voyage to the Otherwordly Islands of the West to discover that he was now the stuff of ancient legend. As one of his crewmen stepped ashore he crumbled to dust. Maelduin crossed a crystal bridge to visit the Isle of Women. The fairy women of the Otherworld, known as the *bean-sidhe* (or banshee), are royally attired and bear wounded heroes away to heal them, just as Morgana bore the dying Arthur away over the water to Avalon where he would be healed and await rebirth as a future king.

# MYTHOLOGICAL ORIGINS

*The Celts held the spoken word in the highest regard, and their myths, legends and traditions were transmitted orally. Although they had no specific creation myth, the legend that human beings were descended from trees, which were also the source of poetry, reflects the deep-seated Celtic sense of interconnection with the natural world.*

### THE IRISH CELTS

There is a well-known mythological sequence giving the story of how the land of Ireland was populated. The first inhabitants, just three men and 51 women, all perished in the great flood of the Old Testament. All that is except for one man, Fintan, who survived by changing himself first into a salmon that swam through the waters, then into a hawk so that he could watch the mountains reappear as the flood drained away.

Invaders then sailed in from the West but fell to fighting among themselves. Their numbers were further diminished when a plague overcame them. Nine survivors of a fleet, lost in the ocean, then settled in Ireland and ruled for many centuries until they were overcome by evil spirits and were either killed or fled. One chief, called Britan, fled to the mainland that now

*LEFT: A nineteenth-century artist's impression of an elaborately dressed Arch Druid.*

bears his name. Others fled to Ancient Greece and eventually returned: among them were the Fir Bolg (possibly Belgae, Celts from Northern France) who, with others, created the five provinces of Ireland. The next invaders were the Tuatha de Danaan, the people of the goddess Danu. They came flying through the air and landed in Ireland on the first day of May.

The magical powers of the Tuatha de Danaan were able to overcome the magic of the evil spirits who lived on an island, and whose demon-king was called Balor. Balor was slain by the spear of Lugh, the warrior-god of the Tuatha, who had first to avenge the death of his father, Kian, who had been killed by the three sons of Turenn. This he did by setting the brothers the task of obtaining the magical weapons needed to defeat Balor.

The Tuatha ruled Ireland until a new race of tall and beautiful people – the Celts – arrived from Spain. They and the Tuatha agreed to divide Ireland between them. The Tuatha would live beneath the ground and the Celts would live above it, and so it has been to this very day.

*LEFT: Irish ollamh and bard.*

men or women and were shamans, mediators, knowers and keepers of wisdom. Like the bards, all their lore was memorized and passed down verbally. They acted as both priests and judges.

## BARDS AND DRUIDS

Next to the king, or warlord, the most important figures in Celtic society were the Druid and the bard or poet. The attainment of the seven grades of a bard lasted twelve years, of which the first six were devoted to memorizing stories, learning grammar, law and what was known as the Secret Language of Poets. In his seventh year he was called anruth or "noble stream". In the last three years he became an ollamh, or doctor, and by the time he had finished his training he knew 100 poems of a type restricted to ollamhs, 120 orations, the Four Arts of Poetry and 350 stories.

The Druids (*drui* in Irish, *derwydd* in Welsh) were seers, with an intimate knowledge of the natural world, who walked between the outer world and Annwn, the Otherworld. They could be either

*RIGHT: A Druid performs the ceremonial cutting of the sacred plant mistletoe.*

# HEROES AND HEROINES

*In every culture, legends evolve about heroes and heroines who are the archetypal characters of the age, the tribe or the race. The Celtic heroes were role-models for the Celtic warrior. They were hard-fighting, hard-drinking, hot-tempered, lustful and boastful, but also passionate, brave and idealistic.*

## LEGENDARY WARRIORS

Finn MacCool, who built the Giants' Causeway for his convenience, and Cuchulainn, the champion warrior of Ulster, who filled his chariot with the heads of his enemies, were both larger-than-life

*ABOVE: Cuchulainn carries Ferdiad across the river.*

*LEFT: Cuchulainn rides into battle.*

142

rowdies. Gilla Stag-shank could clear three hundred acres in one leap, Henbeddestr could outrun men on horseback and Gwaddn Osol could level a mountain by standing on it.

The authority of the Welsh chieftain, Pwyll, even extended into the Otherworld. In order to settle a debt of honour, he changed places for a year with Arawn, king of Annwn, and succeeded in killing a rival who had to be vanquished with a single blow. The code of honour Pwyll followed links him with the heroic figure of King Arthur and the numerous legends of the Round Table which later became popular medieval romances.

## PEERLESS WOMEN

Celtic heroes often learned the arts of war from warrior women and it was the mother who would name and arm the warrior. Cuchulainn, for example, was sent to Skye to learn the arts of war from Scathach, a warrior goddess, and to learn the arts of love from her daughter Uathach.

The heroines of Celtic myths enjoyed power and commanded armies in their own right, as did the historical Queen Boudicea, who led a revolt against Roman rule in first-century Britain. Queen Maeve of Connacht was believed to hold the kingdom's sovereignty in her person, and no king could reign there unless he was married to her. Her most famous action was the invasion of Ulster, when her forces captured the great brown bull of Cuailgne in

ABOVE: *Maeve the Warrior Queen*

the war against Cuchulainn. Emer, Cuchulainn's wife, was said to be blessed with the six gifts of womanhood: beauty, chastity, wisdom, sweet speech, song and needlecraft. But she also demanded that Cuchulainn should improve his fighting skills and prove himself before she could marry him.

# THE MYTHS AND THE SORROWS

*There is both joy and sorrow in Celtic myths which reflect the reality of life,*
*and the Celt is nothing if not a realist.*

A thread of tragedy runs through Celtic mythology: there are many stories of outcasts, doomed lovers and lost children. The love-story of Diarmid and Grainne ends with Diarmid being killed by a wild boar, while both Tristan and Isolt know from the beginning that their love affair is doomed, but are powerless to alter their fate. Deirdre, before she was ever born, was foretold by the Druids to be the ruination of Ulster and, later known as Deirdre of the Sorrows, threw herself to her death from her chariot. As the Celts suffered successive invasions and conquests, their legends reflected the precariousness of the warrior's life, nostalgia for past greatness, and a recognition that adversity must be patiently endured.

### THE STORY OF OISIN AND NIAV

The love-story of Oisin and Niav also ends sadly, but with a twist of humour from the monk who recorded it. Finn MacCool, leader of the Fianna, the warriors who guarded the High King of Ireland, was hunting with his son Oisin by Loch Lene when they saw a lovely girl on a white horse, riding across the waters towards them. She was Niav of the Golden Hair, daughter of the King of Tir Nan Og, the Land of Eternal Youth. She was in love with Oisin and had come to seek his hand in marriage. Oisin fell in love with Niav at once, climbed up behind her, and they galloped off together.

They crossed the ocean and arrived at the Land of Eternal Youth where Oisin was instantly changed into the Ever-Young. He and Niav were married

*LEFT: Deirdre cradles the severed head of her murdered lover.*

and her father left for the Land of Silence. They ruled in his place for timeless centuries, deeply in love, until Oisin began to pine for Ireland, his father, Finn, and his own folk.

Niav lent him her white horse but warned him that his feet must never touch the ground. Oisin rode over the ocean to Ireland, but it was changed and the ancient home of the Fianna was overgrown with grass. Riding back to the sea, he fell from his horse and immediately became the oldest man in the world. But St Patrick was passing by and baptized him, so Oisin died a good Christian and went to heaven.

*ABOVE: Oisin and Niav journey towards the Land of Eternal Youth.*

*RIGHT: Years later on his return, Oisin falls from his horse and instantly loses his magical youth.*

# THE SOURCE OF INSPIRATION

*Wisdom, inspiration and the gift of prophecy could be bestowed by inhabitants of the Otherworld, often in miraculous cauldrons containing magical potions.*

## THE GREAT CAULDRON

Various magical cauldrons crop up again and again in Celtic mythology. Sometimes it was a vessel which fed everyone, at other times it was a huge pot that brought dead warriors back to life. Sometimes the cauldron may have had a part to play in sacrifice and always it was something to be sought through hardship and great peril, possessed and fought over. In Christian times it became the Holy Grail, identified with the Chalice of Jesus's Last Supper.

*LEFT: The Gundestrup cauldron, 1st century AD.*

*BELOW: A detail from the Gundestrup cauldron.*

## GUARDIANS OF THE CAULDRON

The Dagda, the "Good God", is guardian of the Cauldron. Bran, a later god-like chieftain, also has a cauldron. Its properties include an ability to satisfy the hunger and thirst of all and sundry, and to bring the dead back to life. The great poet and prophet, Taliesin, came to his bardic illumination after sipping inspiration – the Celts called it Awen – from the forbidden cauldron of the goddess Ceridwen. Another seer was Myrddin (who appears in the Arthurian stories as Merlin), probably a historical figure of the early Christian period. Having lost his wits following a great battle, his return to sanity seems to owe much to a fairy woman or priestess of Ceridwen.

The cauldron has a significance beyond the Celtic world. The Germanic goddess Nerthus supervised the ritual drowning of her victims and, embossed on the great Gundestrup Cauldron there is a goddess plunging soldiers into it. Is this an act of sacrifice, or is it for bringing them back to life? We don't know for certain.

## WISDOM, MANIPULATION
## AND POWER

Annwn, the Otherworld, was the source of inspiration. It also offered the temptations of manipulation and power. From Annwn, the poets sought Awen, their bardic inspiration, and from Annwn the druids also sought the authority which enabled them to impose *geas* (prohibitions) upon chiefs and kings. Each *geas* carried with it an implied curse: "If you do this, something terrible will happen!" It was a taboo that could apply to the speaking of names, the eating of certain foods, or the participation in a forbidden activity. It was used by the druids as protection – the *geas* represented influence through fear.

Idris was a Welsh giant. With Gwydion, son of Don, and Gwynn, son of Nudd, he was one of the three great astronomers of Britain. He was said to map the heavens and knew the future, until the day of doom. The summit of Cader Idris, or "Idris' Chair", was a dreadful place, for if a man spent the night there he must surely be found, when morning came, either dead, mad, or filled with Awen. This mythology indicates both the temptations and the perils of seeking to penetrate the mysteries of the Otherworld. It also suggests its rewards but includes the warning that death, or madness, lies in wait for the presumptuous.

*RIGHT: Another of the goddesses associated with the legends of Arthur, the Damsel of the Holy Grail.*

# MYSTICISM AND THE LAND

*In Celtic culture, the spiritual and material worlds were interconnected and humanity was part of nature, each being enriched by the other. Poetic inspiration came directly from natural forces.*

An example of this is the Celtic idea of kingship, which depended upon a relationship with the Mother Goddess, a force of nature. This relationship meant that the land did not belong to the people but that the people belonged to the land. There was a sacral, even a nuptial relationship between king and Goddess.

The Celts inherited the traditions and religious practices of older peoples and one of the ways of seeking Awen, or poetic inspiration, was by lying in the dark in a cave or rock chamber, usually at a site regarded as specially potent for the purpose, and

*ABOVE: Rolling Irish hills interact with the flat sea.*

*BELOW: Land and water are joined but distinct.*

awaiting visions and inspirations. It may be that this formed part of an initiatory process.

The bards and the Druids, together with other individuals, put great emphasis on Awen, inspiration and insights from Annwn, the Otherworld, or what might now be described in Jungian terms as the collective unconscious. In the same way the later, Celtic-Christian, mystics sought an eternally loving union with God in mystical prayer. There was no such notion of love between the pagan gods and humanity, however, who were essentially natural forces and archetypes to be known through mythology and to be propitiated out of fear.

*ABOVE: Nature and humanity are as one in the landscape.*

## THE EXPRESSION OF NATURE

The strong sense of identification of Celtic people with the land remains to the present day. It finds expression in music and dance. Dance expresses both earthly and cosmic relationships, and also the mysteries of love and of war. Folk music is an expression of the folk singer's or musician's affiliation with nature and the landscape.

The song of a water sprite, the song of a bird, or the improvisations of a Celtic fiddle player were all regarded as one. Folk music is directly derived from and inspired by nature. Both the song of a bird and the improvisations of a musician are spontaneous and unconscious. Celtic people communicated with each other and their environment through music and dance, as do their descendants today.

*BELOW: An Irish-Celtic standing stone from c. 1st century AD bears continual witness to human behaviour.*

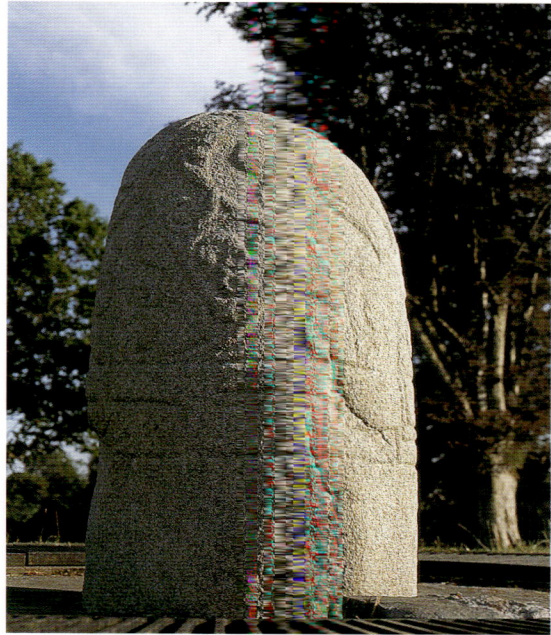

# LOOKING FOR INNER SILENCE

*Celtic mysticism is a timeless appreciation of a reality beyond the everyday, which is
just as relevant today as in the bygone age of Celtic paganism. Its basis is an awareness
of harmony with nature and the unity of Creation.*

Mysticism, in any shape or form, depends upon inner silence and self-awareness. This involves removing external noises and distractions and then trying to remove all the internal noise which modern life stirs up within you. A well-tried Celtic tradition, used by poets until quite recent times, involves lying down in a quiet, darkened room, with a flat stone on the stomach. Choose a time when you know you will not be disturbed so that you feel free to let your mind drift completely. The stone should be just heavy enough to prevent sleep and just light enough not to be positively uncomfortable. With a blindfold over the eyes and silence without, you can begin the task of seeking silence within.

Let a poem arise out of your depths. Don't try too hard. Try not to think. Be as silent as you can and allow words to come to the surface. Keep silent for as long as you can. When the time seems right, come back to the world and write down what came to you. Never mind if it seems half-finished or makes little sense. It is the inner silence that matters and this is an ancient Celtic way of seeking it.

*ABOVE: Shut out the common
light of day.
RIGHT: In a quiet place seek
the silence within.*

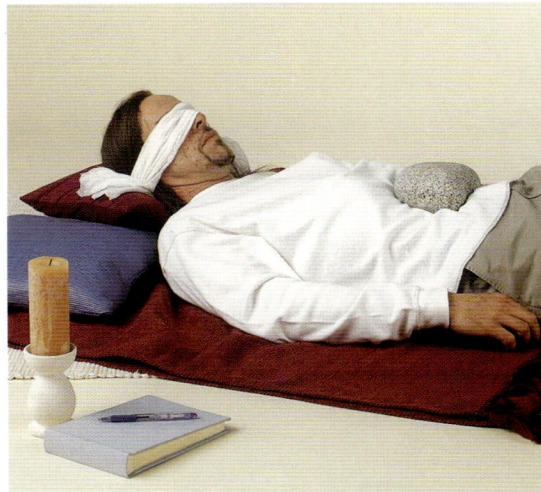

*ABOVE: Return to the light of
day illuminated from within.*

*ABOVE: Experience the touch and texture of a stone.*

*ABOVE: Listen to the wind in the trees and feel the sun.*

*ABOVE: Look closely and enter into the wonder of plant life.*

*ABOVE: Discover the beauty of nature's tiny things.*

## INSPIRATION FROM NATURE

The threads of creation weave together to form a tapestry of great beauty. The art and culture of the Celts reflects their vision of interconnectedness and their drawing of inspiration from the world of nature is something all too often forgotten in modern Western society.

Simply going for a walk can bring you closer to the earth and more in tune with its natural cycles. Meditating under a tree or in a cave can heighten awareness of the totality of which we are a part.

Find a place that is special to you, where you feel a sense of belonging. Be still there and notice what is all about you: trees, grass, water, sky, animals and insects.

Close your eyes and breathe deeply to relax yourself. With your eyes closed you can expand your other senses. Hear the wind in the trees, water lapping, insects moving. Smell the scents carried on the breeze and rising up from all round. Chew a blade of grass and discover its sweetness. Feel the texture of a rock.

Try to extend your senses further. Feel what is beneath the soil, in the sky: roots growing, clouds scudding, the very earth breathing.

When you open your eyes appreciate the experience of being for what it is, both humbling and inspiring.

*RIGHT: Nature is a trans-figured image of its creator.*

# A JOURNEY TO ANNWN

*The Celt looks naturally towards the setting sun. The Gaelic Tir Nan Og is an island in the west. The British Avalon – Island of Apples – belongs to Annwn, the Otherworld. There, Arthur lies, listening to fairy music. Some speculate that Avalon, the grave of Arthur, is that invisible island in Llyn Tegid, where Ceridwen's cauldron was once said to be. There are other contenders for this lost land, but a Celtic tradition continues of a white barge that takes the soul to its home in the Land of Eternal Youth.*

## THE OTHERWORLD

Celtic art and culture reflect the inspiration drawn from nature but inspiration was also sought from Annwn, the place from which they sprang and to which they would return. The Celts, with their sense of universal interconnectedness, saw the Otherworld as an extension of this world which could be reached by various "gateways".

To undertake a shamanic journey in the creative imagination requires little other than an objective to seek and a desire to seek it. You will need to find a place where you won't be disturbed. Spend a while becoming fully recollected and focussing on why you are making this journey and what you hope to find when you reach the Otherworld in your imagination. When you are fully "centred" in yourself, lie down and close your eyes.

You are looking for an entrance into the earth. It might be a cave or a cleft in the rock, a well or a spring, but you will know the entrance to Annwn when you see it.

*RIGHT: The living flame, symbol of light within.*

*RIGHT: Release your mind and let your creative imagination take you on a journey.*

*ABOVE: Return deliberately and extinguish the flame of your candle.*

Enter without fear, but with respect. This is a magical realm where anything is possible. You may meet obstacles, animals or people that bar your way. Use your creative imagination to get round them.

You may meet helpers, who could take any form: people you have known, others you do not recognize, spirits or even gods

*RIGHT: Use the images and tales of the ancient world as inspiration.*

and goddesses. You can also change your own shape or appearance. Be determined in your aim and resourceful in the way that you confront difficulties, don't be frightened or turned aside by anything in your way.

When you return at the end of your journey, focus yourself firmly back into normal consciousness. Go over the journey and write it down. Your concentration will improve the more you practise.

# MEETING THE ARCHETYPES

*The Celtic myths and legends are a tangled web of stories, handed down over untold generations by poets and storytellers, and only recorded in writing less than fifteen hundred years ago. The myths and their characters are archetypal; they originate from our deepest tribal and collective memories. Essentially, they are about humanity. To read the stories and to meet the characters is to meet parts of our own selves, including parts that we may not like very much. Read them and get to know them. They are the foundation upon which great things were built.*

*ABOVE: Druid priestess with sacred mistletoe.*

*LEFT: A druid, a potential source of wisdom, knowledge and inspiration.*
*RIGHT: Morgan le Fay, crafty witch and seductress.*

Archetypes are aspects of ourselves that may hold the answers to what we are seeking. Meeting with an archetype in meditation is a way of gaining access to the unconscious. By giving the unconscious a form, using the creative imagination, it is easier to access and communicate with it. By calling upon a bard or a Druid, a hero or a heroine, insights and strengths can be called up from within ourselves.

## A FORM FOR A MEDITATION

First of all tell yourself, aloud, what you want to do and who you want to meet. Then find somewhere where you will not be disturbed, settle yourself comfortably and breathe deeply to become relaxed.

Visualize yourself in the hall of a Celtic chief. A fire burns in the central hearth and its flickering light illuminates the roof timbers and the thatch. You are seated in a carved chair on a low dais, ready

*ABOVE: Cuchulainn, the archetypal warrior.*

154

*ABOVE: Tell yourself clearly what your intentions are.*

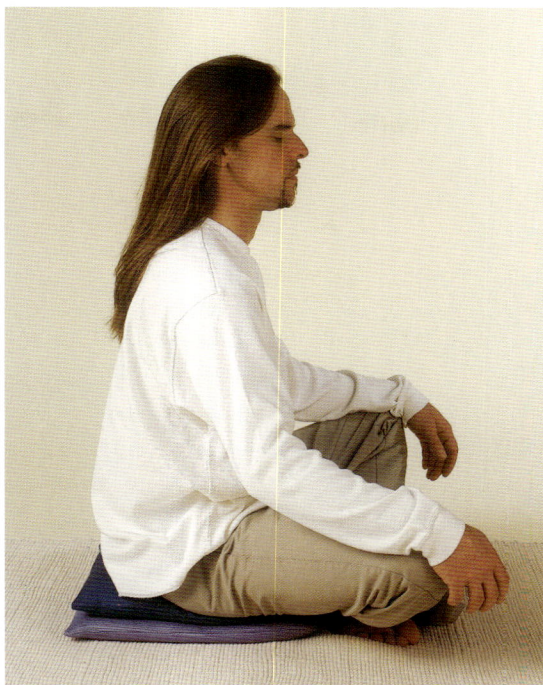

*ABOVE: While the images are clear in your mind, write down what you have learned and return to it in a few days to seek further illumination.*

*RIGHT: Relax, visualize, concentrate on the detail.*

to receive whoever shall come to you. (In other words, you are in control.) When you feel truly there, call on the archetype you want to talk to.

Be courteous when you meet and ask the name of whoever you have called. Tell whoever it is why he or she has been called and what you want of them. Don't forget to thank your archetype when the meeting is concluded.

Return, quite deliberately, to full and normal consciousness (this is important, take some time to ensure that you have achieved this) and write down what you have learned.

Concentration during this kind of meditation can be hard to maintain at first, but it comes with practice. You may find the same archetypes keep returning or you may encounter new ones each time. They may tell you about themselves, and therefore something about yourself at the same time. Treat them with respect as they can be quite formidable, even a bit disturbing. They are connected with human nature, and are therefore quite uninhibited. Meditate on them, talk to them in your imagination, but do not try to force answers from them during your dialogues. They will teach you more than you expect.

# Mysticism

The central part of Celtic mysticism was that faith and life were regarded as one. For Celtic Christians, the perfection of the natural world they saw around them was the ultimate manifestation of God's supreme creative power. God is in all things and all things are in God; the Earth is a living organism, and everything that exists is a potential source of blessing. The whole of life is a continuous experience of the frontier of consciousness between heaven and earth. Daily meditation is a good way of acquiring a mystical habit of mind.

# THE PAGAN CELTS

*Pagan religion has its dark side. There is evidence of human sacrifice, although Roman accounts of this may be more propagandist than reliable. It is a great mistake, however, to regard pagan religion and religious practice as necessarily dark and fear-ridden. Much of it was assimilated, without difficulty, into a later Christianity that was perceived as fulfilling it.*

To see how Christianity was seen and recognized by the Celts as a belief system they could assimilate it is necessary first to explore the pagan beliefs the Celts held in the pre-Christian era. The Great Mother is mother both of the gods and of the Celtic people and the Great Mother is, of course, the Earth Mother herself. As is typical of Celtic deities, she has three names: Anu, Danu and Don. The hills in Kerry, "the Paps of Anu", reflect one aspect, while as Danu she is mother of the Irish gods and as Don she is the

*BELOW: An artist's impression of a pagan Celtic burial.*

ancestor of the British gods. As the Earth Mother is reflected in the landscape, so all sovereignty depends upon the people's relationship with her. The poets adapted the tribal myths to conform to their local landscape in order to establish a sense of authority which was part of the Celtic people's security.

### THE GOOD GOD

The name Dagda means the "Good God". His two other names, Eochaid Ollathair, "Father of All", and Ruadh Rofessa, "Red One of Perfect Knowledge", describe the one who performed miracles and saw to the weather and the harvest. The male deity is a more shadowy figure than the Goddess and there is a confused, and confusing, mythology about him. He is styled King of the Tuatha de Danaan, the pre-Gaelic Irish who now dwell under the Earth.

### THE MORRIGHAN AND BRIGIT

The Morrighan is a formidable female personality, a persona of the Goddess who was the king's champion and protector of the land. The threefold Morrigna – Morrighan and her sisters – appeared at the death of a king or hero, often in the guise of

*ABOVE: An artist's depiction of a Druid sacrifice.*

*RIGHT: Standing stones represent an ancient link between man and gods.*

carrion crows. At Cuchulainn's death, the Morrighan perched on his shoulder as a black crow. The trio of Arthur's half-sisters, including Morgan le Fay, echoed this complex legendary figure.

A more comfortable personality is Brigit, daughter of Dagda and patron of poets, smiths and healers. She was the Fair Maid of Spring and, in the Outer Hebrides, rites of Brigit were known almost within living memory. An image of Brigit as a young maid was dressed in white, a crystal was placed over its heart and it was invited into the house to the singing of songs and ancient chants. These were women's rites, performed at the turn of the Celtic year, and had primarily to do with new birth.

## THE CULT OF THE HEAD

The human head was a symbol for the Celts of divine power and, as the seat of the soul, a link with the ancestral spirits. During times of war the severed heads of enemies were collected and fixed to the doorposts of forts and houses. It was thought that the heads protected the buildings, a belief that persisted well into the medieval period.

The head of the legendary British king, Bran the Blessed, was cut off by his own troops after his defeat in Ireland, and continued to eat and speak during the voyage home. By tradition it was buried in London and still lies under the Tower of London, protecting Britain from invasion.

# RESPECT FOR THE OLD WAYS

*A respect for all that had gone before characterized the relatively speedy conversion of the Celtic people to the Christian faith. Our knowledge of this conversion is centred, in the main, on a large number of outstanding individuals who succeeded, not in arbitrarily abolishing the past and attempting to start again from scratch, but rather in "baptizing" what had gone before.*

## FULFILMENT, NOT CONDEMNATION

"The sober Christianity of Patrick and the wild paganism of the Celts" were, according to one Irish writer, the dual influences on his boyhood. What had gone before was not denied or condemned, it was

*BELOW: Launcelot fights the dragon.*

baptized and fulfilled. If a party of Celtic warriors had turned up for Mass on a Sunday morning, "my eyes would have been surprised, but not my imagination or my faith," he wrote. It was in fact the Celtic Christian monks of the fifth century who had recorded the legends for posterity, because they represented the nature that divine grace would glorify.

*ABOVE: Launcelot by the deathbed of Guinevere.*

Arthur straddles the Celtic and Christian traditions with each claiming him as their own. Arthur was a king caught between the old order and the new. His queen, Guinevere, comes from Annwn, as her name, beginning with "Gwyn" (white), reveals. Her lover, Launcelot (of the Lake – Annwn), is related, mythologically, to the Celtic sun hero. The whole Arthuriad is Celtic mythology, baptized and – in the Grail legends – transformed into a Christian layman's spirituality. Nothing of value is lost.

*ABOVE: The Irish saint, Patrick, a Celtic Christian.*

## COMMUNICATING WITH RESPECT

St Paul preached the Christian gospel in Athens, using a pagan altar inscription as his starting-point. St Patrick did very much the same in Ireland. Patrick had been captured by Irish pirates in his youth and was a slave until he escaped. He returned to Ireland as a bishop. He understood the Irish and their beliefs and, within the space of a lifetime,

Ireland was evangelized. Patrick and his companions knew how to present the Christian faith to them, without compromise but with respect for them and for the best of their old ways.

## CONVERSION BY CHARACTER

What converted Ireland, however, was not Patrick's eloquence but his holiness. He seemed quite different from other men; he knew God as his friend. Patrick is associated with many wild and lonely places in Ireland; places which he loved. Alone with the wild beauty of land, sea and sky all about him, he could lose himself in the Love of God and take it all with him in his heart. This is what the essence of Celtic mysticism is all about.

*BELOW: St Colmcille (Columba) bless his old horse.*

# THE BAPTISM OF A PAGAN GODDESS

*The pagan concepts of deity were not so much denied as corrected. In some cases they were even "baptized". Brigit, as Fair Maid of Spring, was a pagan goddess who inspired affection. Hers was a positive dynamic and she has been assimilated into a historical figure who was probably named after her. Brigit, or Bride, a contemporary of St Patrick, was the daughter of a wealthy pagan, Dubthach, and his bondswoman, Broicsech. Bride became a Christian and dedicated herself to Christ as a nun. Bishop Mel, who received her vocation, is said to have consecrated her as a bishop, claiming divine command, despite the objections of others present. St Bride of Kildare was a Christlike woman, much loved in her lifetime.*

## THE EARTH MOTHER OF GOD

Bride, now a composite figure of Christian saint and pagan goddess, is popularly associated with the Virgin Mary. Her feast day is the Celtic spring festival of Imbolc at the beginning of February, which is also Candlemas, the feast of the Purification of the Blessed Virgin Mary. Celtic Christian mythology has her searching with Mary for the missing boy Jesus in the temple, and she is also said to have been Mary's midwife at the birth of Jesus in the stable at Bethlehem. Such is Bride's association with the Mother of God that she is sometimes called "Mary of the Gaels". The Blessed Virgin herself fulfils all the essential, and necessary, functions of the Earth Mother.

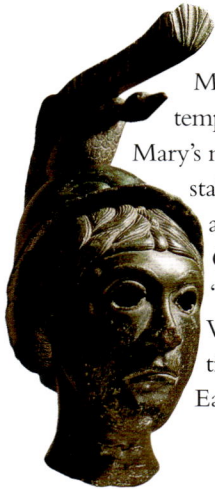

*LEFT: The head of a Celtic goddess.*

*ABOVE: A Holy Well, probably once a Celtic shrine to a pagan god.*

## THE ONCE-PAGAN MIDWIFE OF CHRIST

Bride, baptized by identification with St Bride, may not have been Mary's midwife historically, but in the profoundest sense she was Mary's midwife mythologically. Christians understand the Incarnation as the fulfilment, not only of the Old Testament

*ABOVE: Celtic goddess, child and bird, from the Gundestrup Cauldron.*

*RIGHT: A burial chamber, symbolic of a doorway from this world to another.*

hope, but also of the very best of paganism. The Celts embraced the Christian faith so quickly because it fulfilled them. It did not deny their past but rather baptized it and gave them a new and eternal hope and a personal relationship with God. They continued to revere the natural world but now, instead of existing in its own right, it was seen as the handiwork of God. In this sense, though the Hebrew Mary was acknowledged as the Mother of God, the Celtic Bride was a faithful midwife indeed.

## A NATURAL PROGRESSION

Christian men and women, whose work and witness were seen to be Christ-like, and who had served and often healed their fellow men and women, gradually took the places of the ancient gods in the popular imagination. Wells and other ancient holy places began to be dedicated, no longer to nature spirits, but rather to the local Saint who had often used their waters for baptism and for healing. They remained holy places, dedicated to a personality, not of fear but of love.

# THE CELTIC SUN GOD WALKS THE EARTH

*The Celts, like many pagan and classical religions, included in their pantheon a Sun God whose coming to earth would herald an age of prosperity, health and happiness. Many new converts saw Jesus as fulfilment of this myth, and the dawn of a new order.*

Respect for other people and their beliefs is an obligation of love. The Irish Church was organized around tribal monasteries, and Colmcille, or Columba, (AD521–97), a prince of the northern Ui Neill, became a monk and a great founder of monastic communities in Ireland. He was a noted scholar and scribe who produced a famous copy of the Psalms. However, his family became embroiled in a dispute with the High King Diarmid – of the rival, southern Ui Neill – which ended in the battle of Cul Dreibne, on the slopes of Ben Bulben. Colmcille was implicated and, tormented in conscience, exiled himself to Scotland, sailing with 12 companions across the Irish Sea to the deserted island of Iona, which he made his base. From there he ministered to the Irish enclave of Dal Riada in Argyll and set about preaching the Christian faith in Scotland and the north of England.

On Iona, the formerly hawk-like Colmcille began to live up to his name, which means "dove of the Church". One story tells how, arriving in a pagan community, he said to the chief druid: "Your religion looks forward to a time when the Sun God walks the Earth and all shall be healed. I have good news! He has come, and his name is Jesus."

*RIGHT: St Colmcille, or Columba of Iona.*

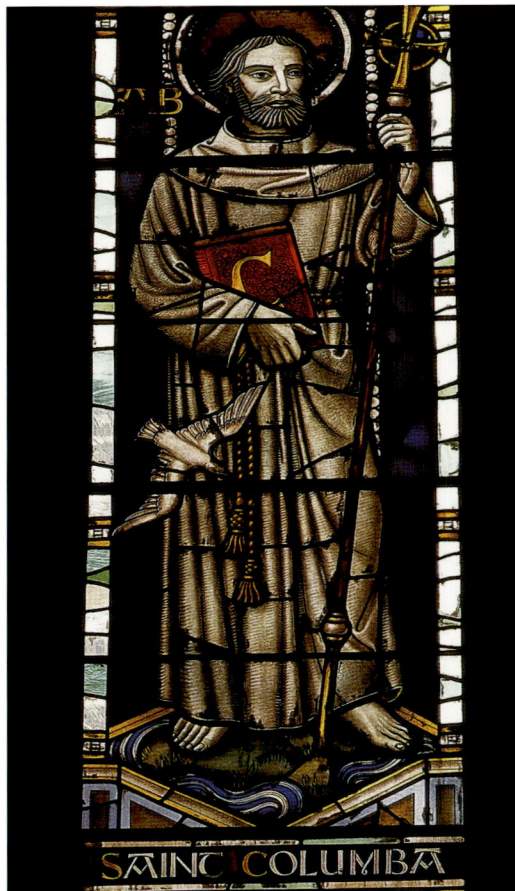

SAINT COLUMBA

*ABOVE: Columba's cell and St Martin's cross, Iona.*

## REASON AND INSPIRATION

Awen, inspiration, is bound up with the human faculty of intuition or the inner "way of knowing". The intuition has to be challenged by reason or a man or woman can become unbalanced in one direction. But reason has also to be informed – and sometimes questioned – by the intuition, or the individual becomes equally unbalanced in the opposite direction; an all too common fault in modern, western society. The Celtic saints reveal a refreshing, and altogether too rare, wholeness.

Colmcille, better known by his Latinized name

Columba, was a very able and accomplished human being. He was a great scholar with a powerful, reasoning mind. But, being a Celt, he was also highly intuitive. He could "see through" people and situations, and he was thought by his followers to possess an uncanny ability to foresee the future. This story of his life shows the otherworldly air that he was thought to have when on one occasion he postponed a fast because he foresaw one was about to visit the monastery and it would have been unkind to expect him to fast. The next day, sure enough, the completely unexpected visitor arrived.

*BELOW: Iona Abbey.*

# LOVE AND RESPECT FOR ALL CREATION

*The transition from paganism to Christianity did not diminish the Celtic
sense of spirituality permeating the natural world.*

A story which typifies the Celts' respect for animal creation is that of Melangell. She may have been Irish or may have been the daughter of a Cumbrian chief. She ran away from her family to escape a forced marriage to another chief. She came to a beautiful little *nant*, or blind valley, in the mountains of Powys, built a hut and lived the life of a Christian hermit. One day Brochwel Ysgithrog, Prince of Powys, was hunting hares. A terrified hare ran from the hounds and hid under Melangell's skirt. The dogs backed off and the huntsman could not command them. Up rode the prince.

"I found sanctuary in this valley and the hare has found sanctuary with me!" said Melangell to Brochwel. He asked for her story and, much moved by her courage and compassion for small creatures, he called off his hounds and graciously gave the *nant* to her as her hermitage. She is buried in the little shrine church at Pennant Melangell and her saintly presence still permeates the whole place.

*ABOVE: St Melangell's
shrine, Powys.*

*LEFT: St Melangell's
Shrine Church, Pennant
Melangell, Powys.*

*ABOVE: Early Celtic Christian saints were often famed for their care and understanding of the animal kingdom.*

It is not surprising to learn that more than one visitor to this remote church has been greeted by a large hare who has led them to the church door before bounding off out of sight.

## RESPECT FOR THE LITTLE THINGS

One of the most attractive personalities of the early Celtic church is Dewi Sant (St David). He founded his monastery at the place which now bears his name when that corner of Wales was under Irish occupation. Dewi's community became a haven of Welsh language and culture, both of which were then under threat. It was said that he spent all of every day, "inflexibly and unwearedly teaching, praying, caring for the brethren and feeding orphans, widows, the needy, the sick, the feeble and pilgrims." He was a tireless founder of Christian communities and, according to legend, provided a hive of bees for each one of them.

One witness said of Dewi that, "He took bread and cress, or water from cold rivers; and wore a full-length horse-hair garment, and did penance beside a spring." Dewi's final message to his followers was: "Brothers and sisters, be happy and keep your faith and your belief, and do the little things that you have heard and seen me do." The little things are the things that really matter, that among other things express respect for all that has gone before.

*RIGHT: A traditional dome-shaped bee hive.*

# PRAYERS AND OFFERINGS

*Prayer, in all its forms, is essentially an expression of a relationship.*
*It is something that is done, not just something that is said.*

Much of pagan prayer was too often an expression of fearful relationships and was propitiatory in character. True prayer, in its widest sense, embraces all manner of relationships: between ourselves and God, between ourselves and the saints, the angels and the faithful departed and between ourselves and the rest of creation. Like the ancient Celtic myths, Gaelic prayers and incantations were transmitted orally, so

*BELOW: Votive offerings, Medron Holy Well, Cornwall.*

that their immediacy and relevance was passed on.

Around the holy wells and holy places in Ireland remarkable collections of small objects may be found, left there by individuals who have prayed there. The leaving of a token, "a little something", is an instinctive courtesy, a symbol that the relationship has been expressed. It is a very human gesture and it is found in many different traditions around the world. In Christian churches it is found in the lighting of votive candles, in folk traditions it can be seen in various local customs, but it can also be a personal ritual that is devised and carried out by an individual. Leaving an offering is a satisfying gesture to make, expressive of both respect and affection. It is also an important part of human life, a recognition of the ebb and flow of energy in the relationship between the human world and heaven. It shows that an exchange has taken place, and is also an expression of gratitude. It matters little what the token is, as long as it is something that has meaning for you.

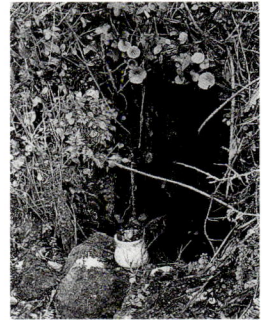

*ABOVE: Holy Well, Alsia, Cornwall.*

## MAKING AN OFFERING OUTSIDE

If you pray indoors, you might like to set aside a particular place as a permanent shrine and leave your offering there. If you pray out of doors leave the token at the base of a tree, or on a rock. Christian believers might use an icon or a cross as their focal point for prayer; but all will have their own personal ways of focussing. Prayer, rightly understood, is a universal activity.

Find a place where you can feel a spiritual connection. Hold the chosen token in your left palm, offer it up to the sky and down to the Earth, and to the four Airts – the four quarters or cardinal points – and allow your heart to feel thankful.

Speak your gratitude aloud, to reinforce your intent, then place the offering on your temporary shrine or in the place you have chosen.

*ABOVE: It matters little what the offering is as long as it has meaning for you. Salt is a long-used token.*

To complete the ritual, complete it in the traditional way by drawing a circle in the air above the offering with your hand and then quartering the circle with a cross.

*BELOW: Offer the token to the Sky, to the Earth and to the Four Airts.*

*BELOW: With care and reverence, place the token in the place you have chosen.*

*BELOW: With two fingers, sign the circle and the cross to complete the ritual.*

# SEEKING GRACE

Mystical experience is generally understood as direct, intuitive knowledge of God or ultimate reality, attained through personal experience. In the Celtic vision, heaven and earth are inextricably intertwined and it is possible that there is no essential distinction to be made between living creatures or supernatural beings. Similarly, from the earliest times, Christians have used the word grace to describe the transforming power of God – the Holy Spirit – within a human soul. The work of grace is to take what is already present in the human spirit, and bring it to fulfilment on a wholly other level of being.

# CREATION IN THE IMAGE OF ITS CREATOR

*For Celtic Christians, the perfection of the natural world they saw around them*
*was the ultimate manifestation of God's supreme creative power.*

A Welsh poet wrote of the sweetness of nature, buried in black winter's grave, and then, in spring, spoke of the willow, whose harp had hung silent, giving forth its melody. "Listen!" he cried, "The world is alive!" An Irish bard sang of a storm at sea, of the ocean's wild, troubled sleep, and of the hair of the wife of Manannan (the sea god), being tossed about. Another poem has news for us of the coming of winter: the stag is calling, cold has seized the bird's wing. The whole of nature is alive, it is all of an unutterable beauty and it is nothing less than the glorified image of its creator.

The Celtic poets of the Dark Ages and the early medieval period wrote of nature with both love and a deep awe. An Irish hermit described his hut in the woods, known only to himself and God. He wrote of the heather, the honeysuckle, the stags, the birds, "the grave and peaceful host of the country-side" all about his door, all for him to love, and in all of whom he found God, "All the gift of my dear Christ."

## THE CELTIC VISION OF NATURE

The Celtic vision derives from a paganism which found its fulfilment by assimilation into the Christian faith. There remains an awareness that the Celts belong to the land, the land does not belong to them. The land is associated with the Goddess, the Earth Mother, however remote this

*LEFT: A stag in autumn heralding the change of season.*

172

*ABOVE: Spring blossom.*

intuitive awareness and the fullest exercise of reason. Where reason is exalted at the complete expense of the intuitive faculty there is no possibility of mysticism, and neither is any true mysticism possible where reason is abandoned. A true mysticism demands equilibrium, a balance of the faculties and an openness to the suits of things. Mysticism must always keep its feet on the ground.

*BELOW: Snowdrops in the snow.*

may be from conscious awareness. Mary, the Mother of God, and her mythical companion, Bride, maintain this connection. A "marriage" of Heaven and Earth brought forth the Incarnation and thus both the biblical and the pagan hopes were fulfilled.

Mysticism depends on the mind being receptive to such a connection. Such a mind is open to both

173

# RELIGION INTERWOVEN WITH LIFE

*There is no separation of religion from life in Celtic spirituality. God is in all things and all things are in God; the Earth is a living organism. Heaven is invisible but is all about us and everything that exists is a potential source of blessing. It is as natural to wish for the Heavenly Host to be seated at one's own table as it was natural for publicans and sinners to invite Christ himself to eat with them, and in both cases the invitation was accepted through love.*

## A CEILIDH FOR THE KING OF HEAVEN

An Irish poet, seeing himself as a tenant of his Lord, the King of Heaven, sought to pay his legal dues of lodging and hospitality. He wrote of his longing to give a great ale-feast for the King of Heaven, and for all the Heavenly Host to be seated at his table forever, feasting and drinking to their hearts' content. He wanted Jesus Christ never to leave the feast, and for the "Three Marys" to grace it with their presence also. He wanted forever to be rent-payer to the Lord and to be able to pay his dues with all the hospitality of his heart.

*BELOW: Jesus feasting at the wedding at Cana, the Celtic ideal of a lord feasting with his followers.*

*ABOVE: A monolith in Co Kerry, Ireland.*

## THE VISION OF WHOLENESS

There is nothing slight or sentimental about Celtic spirituality, it is grounded in a deep realism. It is quite wrong to romanticize it or to imagine that all things were at all times nothing but sweetness and light. Nor are all Celts themselves necessarily natural mystics; true mystics are rare in any generation. What is distinctive about Celtic

*RIGHT: Irish gold torque, c. 1st century BC.*

spirituality, as it has evolved through the centuries from paganism to a mature Christian faith, is its realism. It is close to nature and open both to intuition and to reason. There is a sense of unity between all the elements of life: the angels, the saints, the farmer and his cow.

The Celtic world was shielded by force of historical circumstances from influences which over the years tended to obscure the Church's vision of this holistic approach. There is, for example, nothing of the disturbed and disturbing equation

*BELOW: A romantic nineteenth-century impression of druid women dancing round the menhir.*

*ABOVE: Earth and the vault of the heavens.*

of sex with sin, or an implication that material creation is in some way imperfect, which have hung about the edges of the Church's mind, though wholly foreign to the teaching of the gospel. Celtic spirituality is essentially primitive and rooted in a oneness with nature

# HEAVEN INTERWOVEN WITH EARTH

*Heaven permeates earth and earthly life in the Celtic vision. The whole of life – as recorded in hymns, incantations, prayers and even magic spells – is a continuous experience of the frontier between heaven and earth. This is a frontier of consciousness, not a physical line drawn on the ground. The character of heaven is not that of Annwn, one of darkness tinged with fear, it is one of light, life and above all, love.*

*LEFT: The Archangel Michael defeats Satan.*

## INTERWOVEN REALITIES

Heaven, though unseen, is all about us. Day-to-day life is lived in the context of a heaven which is only just out of normal human sight. The fisherman asks that the king of the elements, Christ himself, be seated at the helm. The mystery of seed-sowing is celebrated with its own *ortha*, or incantation. The sower will go round his field sun-wise, with the angels and the apostles for company and in the full sight of the Blessed Trinity. He will begin his harvest on the feast of the Archangel Michael and raise the first cut of the sickle, turning it three times round his head in honour of the Trinity.

## HEAVEN AT HOME

Mary and Bride encircle the hearth, the floor and the entire household. The holy apostles are present, unseen. By the bed is Bride and her fosterling, the Christ-Child. The Mother of God watches over the household and Christ himself, the king of the sun, is always at your shoulder. A morning song must be sung to God, for Mary's lark is singing it in the clouds and every other living creature is singing its song of love. Will you alone be dumb?

The Mother of God, the holy Archangel Michael and "gentle Bride of the locks of gold" are invoked to "keep my feet on the just path." Heaven is completely interwoven with earth. The darkness of Annwn is lit up by the light of heaven.

## THE ANGELS AND THE COW

A *sain* (blessing) is placed upon sheep, with the sign of the cross, as protection against all that may harm them. Cattle are entrusted to the care of St Columba, St Brigit (Bride) and Mary the Mother of God. When the cattle come home they are met with a song of welcome, *failte a' chruidh*, to which they respond, sometimes lowing, sometimes bellowing. This is to acknowledge that the Three Persons of the Blessed Trinity have kept the precious cattle from harm and brought them safely home. At the milking, the aid of the angels and the saints is asked to persuade the young cow to take to her calf.

ABOVE: *Another battle between good and evil as Michael casts down the devil.*

The others are of great antiquity. The incantations or chantings assimilated the piety of pagan Celts and transformed them. They were passed down orally from generation to generation and were only collected and recorded in the 19th century. They represent a genuine mysticism of the hearth, a religious sense of ceremony that is woven into everyday life.

## PEARLS AND SWINE

It has been said that "the mind is the slayer of the real." Our faculty of reason is quick to rationalize and to try to "explain away" anything that is out of the ordinary. A deep, inner experience, be it psychical in nature or mystical is quickly "psychologized", and thus denied, by many other people who do not share the same awareness. Jesus referred to this when he warned his listeners not to "cast pearls before swine." The pearls are the inner realities, the inner experiences and awarenesses that we are given, which are self-authenticating by virtue of their essential character.

# MAKING PILGRIMAGES

*The word pilgrimage suggests the making of a considerable physical effort. Present-day pilgrimages often involve long walks over many days. This is a valuable exercise for all concerned, for the journey (an touras) is inward as much as it is outward. Once this fact is grasped, then it is possible to make pilgrimages involving considerable inward journeys but quite small outward manifestations of them. Pilgrimage, like mysticism, is first of all the attitude of a mind firmly fixed within the heart. A periodic journey to the heart, perhaps a daily journey, is a good way of acquiring a mystical habit of mind.*

## LOOK FOR THE SMALLEST THINGS

Eternity, said the poet, is in a grain of sand. Make a point of looking for the smallest things: the tiniest flower, the minute details of lichen, the patterns created in nature, especially the smallest ones. Look at minute creatures with a new eye and learn to wonder at them. Look at your own hand and try to realize that if you were looking at it through a microscope powerful enough, it would look like a universe of infinitesimal stars with unimaginable spaces between them. We are made of energy, held together by an intention. Make small regular

*LEFT: A fifteenth-century manuscript showing the progression of a pilgrimage in France.*

*RIGHT: Pilgrim's Path, Nevern, Pembrokeshire.*

*RIGHT: A depiction of the god-dess of day and night.*

pilgrimages in search of tiny things. Remember Dewi Sant's (St David's) advice: "Do the little things." On a starry night, try to escape the light-pollution and the noise-pollution of the town and sit silently, listening to the stars. Think it possible and you will succeed. Remember that the ancient Celts perceived the stars as living creatures.

## TO MAKE A PILGRIMAGE

Sit silently with your spine straight and your head erect. Concentrate your imagination on drawing your mind down into your heart on an inward journey.

If necessary, whisper a short word such as "love" to keep distracting thoughts from flooding in. This will act like cats' eyes in the road when driving on a foggy night.

*LEFT: Look out for and honour the little things.*

A single word, uttered every so often, will keep you out of the ditch of distraction.

Imagine holding your mind in your heart's silence for as long as you can, and then come quietly back to normal consciousness.

Don't try to intellectualize things, just learn to let them be what they are. This is an important part of learning the lifetime's task of letting yourself be what you really are and not what you think you are.

*BELOW: Imagine an inward journey into your heart.*

# NATURE AND GRACE

*Christians from the earliest times have used the word grace to describe the transforming power of God the Holy Spirit within a human soul. The work of grace is to take what is already present in the human spirit, that of nature, and bring it to fulfilment on a wholly other level of being.*

Grace recreates from within; needless to say it does so only with the soul's fullest co-operation and it is at the very least a lifetime's work. Psychism is a natural gift in everyone, though it remains dormant in many. It belongs to nature. The work of grace is to transform psychism to another level altogether,

*BELOW: The meeting of this world and the world of the fairies is often a theme in the Arthurian legends.*

from Annwn to heaven, or mysticism. Fairies may be good but angels are better.

Mysticism belongs, we might say, to the "grace level" of things and not to the "nature level". Bringing the mind into the heart is a work of the human will, aided by grace. It is grace which opens our eyes and enables us to see things in a new way. It allows us to forget ourselves in contemplation of the wonder and beauty of nature all about us through which we gain an insight into the true nature of life. True mysticism is a gift of grace, working with our own little efforts and best intentions.

## CELTIC REALISM

Dewi Sant (St David) realized the need for attention to detail when he said "Do the little things." If the little things are done the big things take care of themselves. This is Jesus' teaching in the gospels and it illustrates the realism which characterizes Celtic spirituality. Dewi gave a hive of bees to each of his foundations so they would have honey, but they would also have living creatures to care for. The Celts adapted church structures to fit the way they actually lived: the Irish monasteries were tribal, and the Welsh Llans were ideal for caring for scattered rural communities.

*ABOVE: The world of fairies.*

## SELF-DISCIPLINE

Anyone who aspires to a mystical approach to life must be ready for a radical change of heart, mind and vision. It will have repercussions on both life and lifestyle. New priorities and habits of self-discipline must be acquired. True self-discipline is a gift of grace and must be asked for, as our natural tendency is to take the soft option and settle for the second best. Self-seeking can sometimes be highly motivated and fiercely self-disciplined in the service of self-interest, but mysticism has nothing to do with getting and everything to do with giving of the self, which is never easy.

An Irishman, possibly a priest, wrote angrily of the clerics beginning to arrive in Ireland from Europe. To his eyes they lacked the ruggedness and the self-discipline of their Irish predecessors. "Silk, satin and featherbeds!" he snorted 'Mitres, rings and chessboards!" How unlike their Irish predecessors of old, "They were not overweight." The old priests had been roughly dressed mildly and with wild haircuts, but they were men of keen learning and their natures were pure. They had "very rough monastic rules", which to order community life, but also encouraged self-discipline, without which any spiritual, or material undertaking fails absolutely.

*BELOW: The spirit of the night*

# MYSTICAL EXPERIENCE

*Mysticism, or more correctly mystical experience, is generally understood as direct, intuitive knowledge of God or ultimate reality, attained through personal experience.*

It is generally recognized that the authenticity of mystical experience is dependent solely on the quality of life that follows the experience. "By their fruits ye shall know them," said Jesus, and there are, in any generation, spurious or pathological "mystical experiences" which are revealed for what they are by the

*BELOW: A hermit, extending his faith through learning.*

*ABOVE: Buddhism stems from mystical experience.*

quality of life that follows upon them. Many great world religions, such as Buddhism and Islam, derive from the mystical experiences of their founders.

True mystical experience is something that is given; it cannot be induced and any experiences which are simply the product of attempts to induce them are almost certainly bogus. Mysticism is not about looking for experiences, it is about acquiring an attitude of heart and mind which sees more profoundly and enters into the wonder and beauty of creation. It knows creation to be the transfigured image of the creator. Mysticism is essentially about learning to love.

*ABOVE: Artistic interpretation plays a part in extending the mystical experiences of established religion.*

## ULTIMATE REALITY

Every world religion has its own distinctive mystical tradition. The direct, intuitive experience of ultimate reality requires to be communicated, for it is never given just for the benefit of the recipient. It is communicated in terms of the language and thought forms of the p████████████. True mystics nearly always find that t██y ██ ████y in tune with each other, whatever t██ ██i█ o█. Perhaps the closest and most fruit██l ███o███ ██tween world religions in recent de████ ██s ██en that between Christian and Buddhi█t ██████a█ve monks.

The Celtic tradition █ ██o██y mystical in that it has an innate awar██o█ ██ ██ ██ity of things, of the need for reali███ ██ ███ ██ equilibrium between the two hu██ ██u██ of reason and intuition. In terms o█ ██ ████mporary Celtic world, some Christia█ ██i██ ████tions are more traditionally Celtic i█ ██i ██████h than others. The Reformed trad███o█ ██ ████ rationalistic and tend to be suspi██o█ ██ ███i██on, others are more comfortable with █.█ ███ █v██t there should be no confusion betw███ ██ ███ ██d Annwn.

*BELOW: St Dwynwen's Cr████ ████y.*

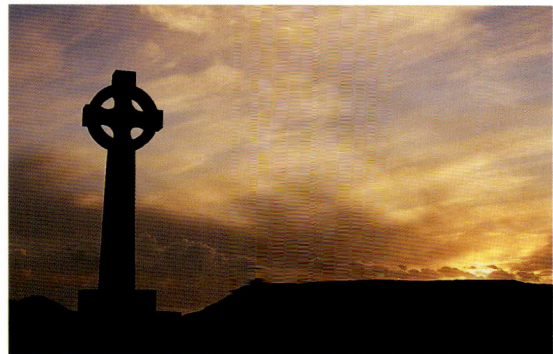

# GOD IS LOVE

*The Christian experience, expressed in the poetic idiom of doctrine,
is that the Trinity consists of three Persons, not three aspects of the deity.*

Examples of triple gods and goddesses are to be found all over the world and even today they exist in aspects of Shivite Hinduism. Celtic paganism was familiar with the idea of triple gods or goddesses, all aspects of the one essential being. To the pagan Celt, therefore, the Christian experience of ultimate reality as a Trinity was not too extraordinary, but the difference is actually profound. The mystery of the Trinity introduces the concept of a personal relationship between three separate individuals. What Christians are saying is that "God is love", but also that God is a love-affair.

*LEFT: William Blake's paintings express a personal experience of God.*

Celtic Christianity is strongly Trinitarian. The Ortha nan Gaidheal is full of invocations of the Three, and seldom is one mentioned without the others, for God is one and three. God is "The High King of Heaven" and as such may be any or all of the persons. It is the sense of personal relationship within the mystery of Godhead that is the guarantee of divine love, for God could not be love, as St John tells us, were God not first of all a love-affair.

## THE RUGGED MYSTICS

Many rocky islets lie just off the west coast of Ireland and on many of them are to be found the remains of a cluster of beehive-shaped stone huts, often surrounded by a dry stone wall. Some of these, put together without mortar, are still almost as their last occupants left them. Some, as on Skellig Michael, appear to cling to a ledge on a bare rock in the middle of the ocean. How could anyone live there?

*LEFT: St Kevin's Cell, Glendalough, Ireland.*

ABOVE: St Govan's Chapel, Pembrokeshire.

RIGHT: Celtic monastery, Skellig Michael, Co. Kerry.

And who did? They were the Culdees, Christian monks, living a life entirely devoted to prayer. Why? Because they were in love with the love of God.

Here is Celtic mysticism at its most rugged. The Culdees were called to such extremes of self-sacrifice, not just for themselves but for others. They sought to diminish the separation between

RIGHT: The distinctive beehive-shaped stone huts of the Culdees.

the spiritual and physically undergoing spiritual exercises which involved great hardship. It was their part to serve their fellow men and women by holding them before God in prayer and, as far as possible, forgetting all about themselves. There were other hermits, men and women, who lived in gentler places and were also filled with love of God in creation, love of creation and all its creatures in God.

# A MIND IN THE HEART

*Mysticism is, first and foremost, an attitude of mind in the heart, and the essential integration of heaven and earth is a reality built into the Celtic vision.*

The Celtic mind is revealed both in its pagan past and in its Celtic Christian faith. It is a mind which thinks all things possible. It is possible that heaven and earth are inextricably intertwined. It is possible that there is no essential distinction to be made between the farmer, his cow, the saints and the

*RIGHT: A holy offering of simple loaves of bread.*

holy angels. It is possible that Bride – once a god-dess, now identified with a Christian saint – is a close friend in heaven of the Mother of God. It is possible that the Celtic saints and the holy angels care for mortal men and women and respond, as friends, to their prayers for help. For love, all things are possible.

Because all things are believed to be possible, they are. There is nothing to fear in the old Celtic pagan-ism. Its perversions (such as cruel sacrifice) have been done away with and its insights affirmed and taken up into the true faith. There is nothing to fear because "perfect love casteth out fear" and instead of the past being denied and demonized it has been affirmed and baptized. What might once have been described as superstition, if ever it was, is regarded now as poetry still trying to express the mystery.

*LEFT: The Sleeping Earth and the Waking Moon.*

186

*RIGHT: Chapel of Our Lady and St Non, St David's, Pembrokeshire.*

## A QUESTION OF ATTITUDE

Mysticism, the attitude of a mind in the heart, is as much as we can aspire to. Celtic tradition can point the way especially to minds that have grown tired with over-full lives, urban stress, noise-pollution and all the mind-pollution that the excessive exposure to the media and modern life in general can induce. Celtic spirituality, or mysticism if you prefer, can be a powerful corrective to the strident, the sickly sentimental and the excessively rationalist, all of which are sometimes to be encountered in contemporary Christianity. Increasingly, those who feel they have lost their way turn to their roots, for many, these roots are Celtic before they are anything else.

*LEFT: A mountain reflected in a dewdrop.*

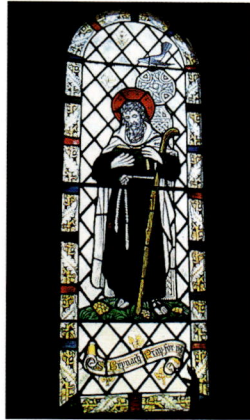

"May the blessing of the rain be on you – the soft sweet rain. May it fall upon your spirit so that all the little flowers may spring up and shed their sweetness on the air. May the blessing of the great rains be on you, that they beat upon your spirit and wash it fair and clean and leave there many a shining pool where the blue of Heaven shines, and sometimes a star. May the blessing of the Earth be on you – the great round Earth. And now may the Lord bless you, and bless you kindly."
(An old Irish blessing.)

*BELOW: Celtic spirituality is reliant on light.*

# THE FESTIVALS OF THE CELTIC YEAR

*The seasons of the year, the solstices, the equinoxes and the cross-quarterings, provided the succession of Celtic festivals, most of which are still celebrated in the calendar of the Christian church. The earth was recognized as a living entity and its cycles were, and still are, reflected in the pattern of human lives, particularly in respect of planting, growth, harvesting and introspection.*

Human and animal life begins in the darkness of the womb, so the day traditionally begins at sunset (as, liturgically, it still does) and the Celtic year begins with the coming of the dark.

SAMHAIN, beginning on the eve of 1st November, is a lunar festival and the Celtic new year. It is the time when such cattle as could not be wintered were slaughtered. It is celebrated by the Church as the major feast of All Saints, beginning liturgically

*BELOW: Cattle brought down from the hills for winter.*

*RIGHT: Chopping wood on a medieval farm.*

on Hallowe'en, in other words the "eve of all Hallows".

YULE, beginning on the eve of 21 December, is a solar festival when the sun, at its weakest, begins to gather strength. The Yule log is a pre-Christian survival; the Church (until recent revisions) marked Yule with the feast of St Thomas the Apostle. Deep pre-Christian instincts cause Christmas carols to be generally preferred before 25 December (originally the Roman feast of the sun god) rather than after Christmas, as would be liturgically correct.

IMBOLC, the time of the lactation of ewes, is a lunar festival beginning on the eve of 1st February, and is the first day of the Celtic spring. It is celebrated as the feast of St Bride of Kildare and, on 2 February, as the feast of the purification, or the presentation of Christ in the temple.

*ABOVE: Resting at harvest time.*

OSTARA, the spring equinox and a solar festival, begins on the eve of 21 March. It is closely associated with Lady Day, the feast of the annunciation on the 25th, once celebrated as New Year's Day.

BELTANE, beginning on the eve of 1 May, is the first day of the Celtic summer and an ancient lunar fertility festival, representing the marriage of the complementary powers of masculine and feminine. It is celebrated as the feast of the apostles St Philip and St James.

COANHAIM is the summer solstice, a solar festival, beginning on the eve of 21 June. It is closely associated with the Feast of the Nativity of St John the Baptist on 25 June.

LUGHNASADH, the last lunar festival of the year, begins the season of harvest and hunting. It begins on the eve of 1 August and is traditionally celebrated as Lammas (or loaf-mass) Day, giving thanks for the first fruits of harvest, when the ceremonial first loaf was baked.

HERFEST (from which the word "harvest" probably derives) was the final solar festival of the year, beginning on the eve of 21 September. Harvest homes and thanksgivings are traditional survivals from pagan times and even today are celebrated around the world. The feast of St Matthew, Apostle and Evangelist, is also celebrated on 21 September. The feast of St Michael and All Angels, on 29 September, is also closely associated.

*BELOW: Lammas Day, enjoying the first fruits of harvest.*

# INDEX